Cockatiels For Two

"*Never, ever, think outside the box.*"

Cockatiels For Two

A Book of Cat Cartoons

by Leo Cullum

Harry N. Abrams, Inc., Publishers

Project Manager: Christopher Sweet
Editor: Sigi Nacson
Designer: Robert McKee
Production Manager: Kaija Markoe

Library of Congress Cataloging-in-Publication Data

Cullum, Leo.
Cockatiels for two : a book of cat cartoons /
by Leo Cullum.
p. cm.
Includes bibliographical references and index.
ISBN 0-8109-4966-0 (hardcover)
1. Cats—Caricatures and cartoons.
2. American wit and humor, Pictorial. I. Title.

NC1429.C84A4 2004b
741.5'973—dc22
2004003432

Printed and bound in China

10 9 8 7 6 5 4 3 2 1

ABRAMS

Harry N. Abrams, Inc.
100 Fifth Avenue
New York, N.Y. 10011
www.abramsbooks.com

Abrams is a subsidiary of

LA MARTINIÈRE
GROUPE

"...and how do you feel once you've had a hissy fit?"

For Kathy

"Where's the canary?"

"*Normally I hate technology but* that *I like.*"

Introduction

Four thousand years ago, ancient Egyptians domesticated the cat and once something has been screwed up for that long it's hard to fix. Actually I'm a little surprised they were able to accomplish it at all. It's easy to picture a prehistoric wolf relaxing in the glow of a campfire and snatching scraps of mastodon, but a cat is either fleeing or attacking, not crouching in the shadows eavesdropping on cave gossip.

It follows that the cat had to have been captured first and then tamed and there has been an underlying current of resentment ever since. This is not true with kittens but once they're grown and have heard all the old tales, there it is, that slight chilliness, the mocking disdain we mistake for independence and self-sufficiency.

Cats tolerate us, and even, on a one-on-one basis, seem to like us. They accept our food, but will bring home a dead rat to show they don't need us at all. Still we love them and wish they would just get over it.

Once these early cats were tamed they provided a tremendous benefit to the farmers, controlling pests in the fields of grain. Hieroglyphics tell of one particularly precocious, if conflicted, cat known as "the ratcatcher in the rye." Their importance was such that they were considered sacred. Puzzle buffs will immediately notice that "sacred" is an anagram for "scared"… thus "scaredy cat." (More on this later, or perhaps not.)

Domestic cats reached Europe in the fourth century A.D., courtesy of the early merchant ships. This was a boon to all concerned as Europe was full of rats. Ask anyone. The Pied

Piper couldn't be everywhere, even with a Eurail pass. Cats then came to the New World with the pilgrims, and eventually, drawn by the faint aroma of sushi borne on the westerly winds, led the settlers to California.

A descendant of these cats lives with us. She is small and wiry, about twelve years old, and, having been born in the wild, is very wary—a master of camouflage and concealment. My daughters named her "Biscuit" because if you had a biscuit shaped like a cat, it might, in a general way, resemble this particular cat.

She makes little chirping noises, purrs, bites if you stop petting her and, to the truly perceptive, has expressive eyes (which frequently express contempt). She comes and goes as she pleases and, except for a standing dinner engagement around seven, does whatever she wants, which is usually sitting primly, her little cat's feet tucked in close, thinking back to the good old days by the pyramids when people would have known she was a goddess...a goddess in a flea collar.

Except for the mouse thing you can't ask much of a cat. They won't pull a sled, herd sheep, lead the blind, bite burglars, rescue mountaineers, fetch the paper, guard a junkyard, point out pheasant, or track escaped convicts. They just won't. If it were merely about pest control we could all keep barn owls.

So what is their appeal? After doing exhaustive research and pondering the question for the better part of the last two days, I've come to a scientific conclusion. The answer is kittens. They are just so darned cute.

—*Leo Cullum, 2004*

"There's more than one way to skin your husband."

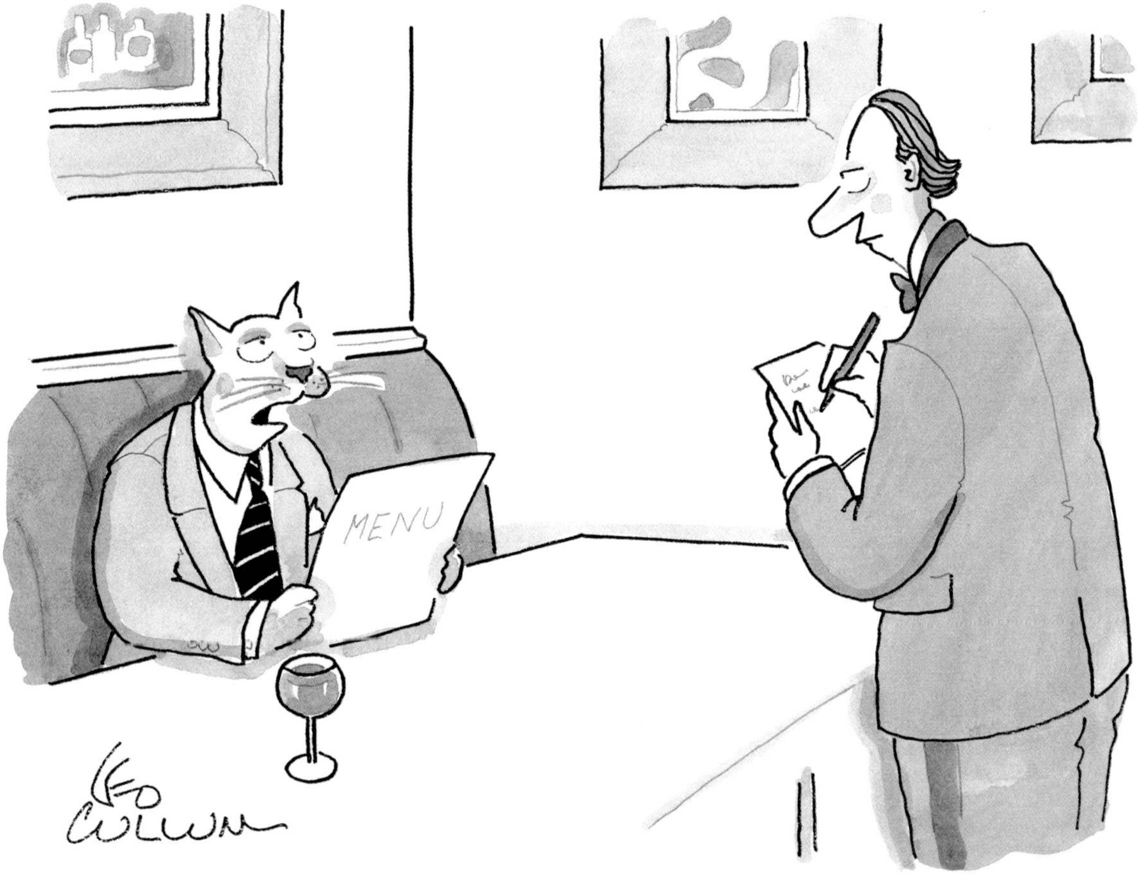
MENU

"Instead of potatoes may I have extra mice?"

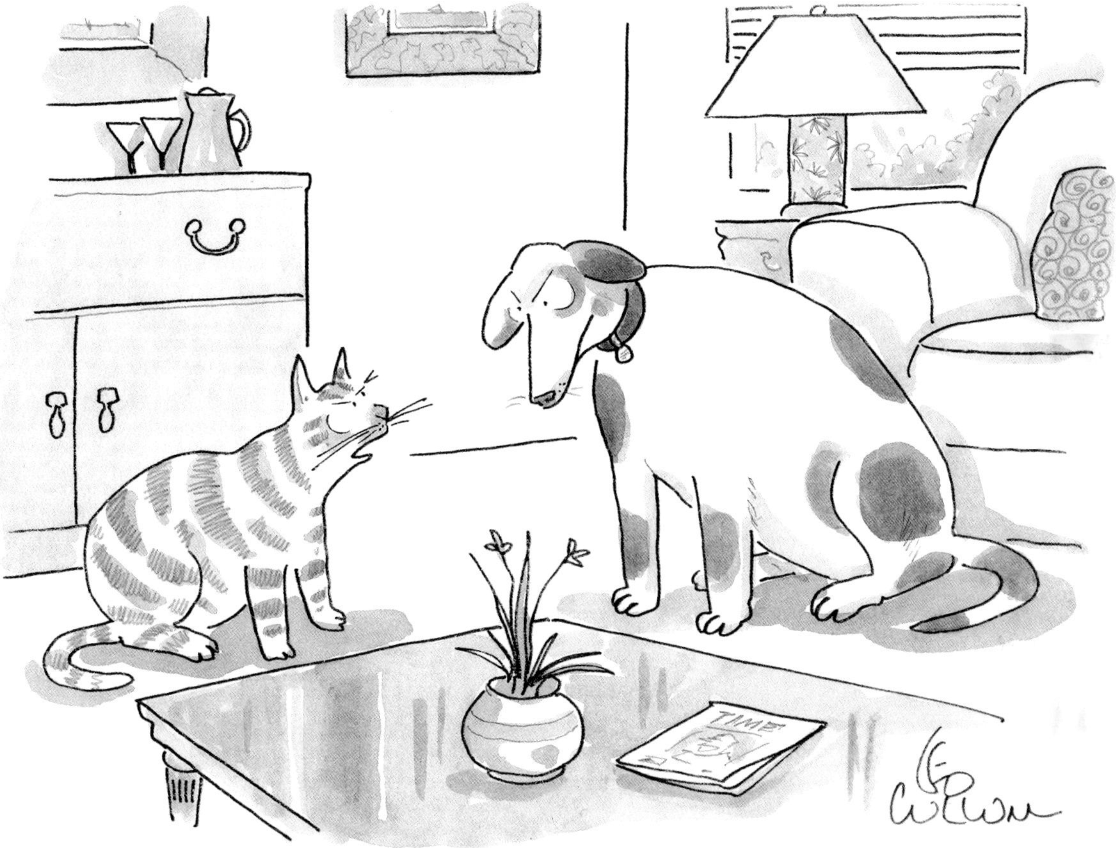
TIME

"O.K., your mouth may be clean but I'll bet your mind is filthy."

"It has to be the chase, because, face it,...mice don't taste that good."

"Hold my calls, Betty. I'm with a ball of string."

"*I'm totally bipartisan. I eat as many birds as I do mice.*"

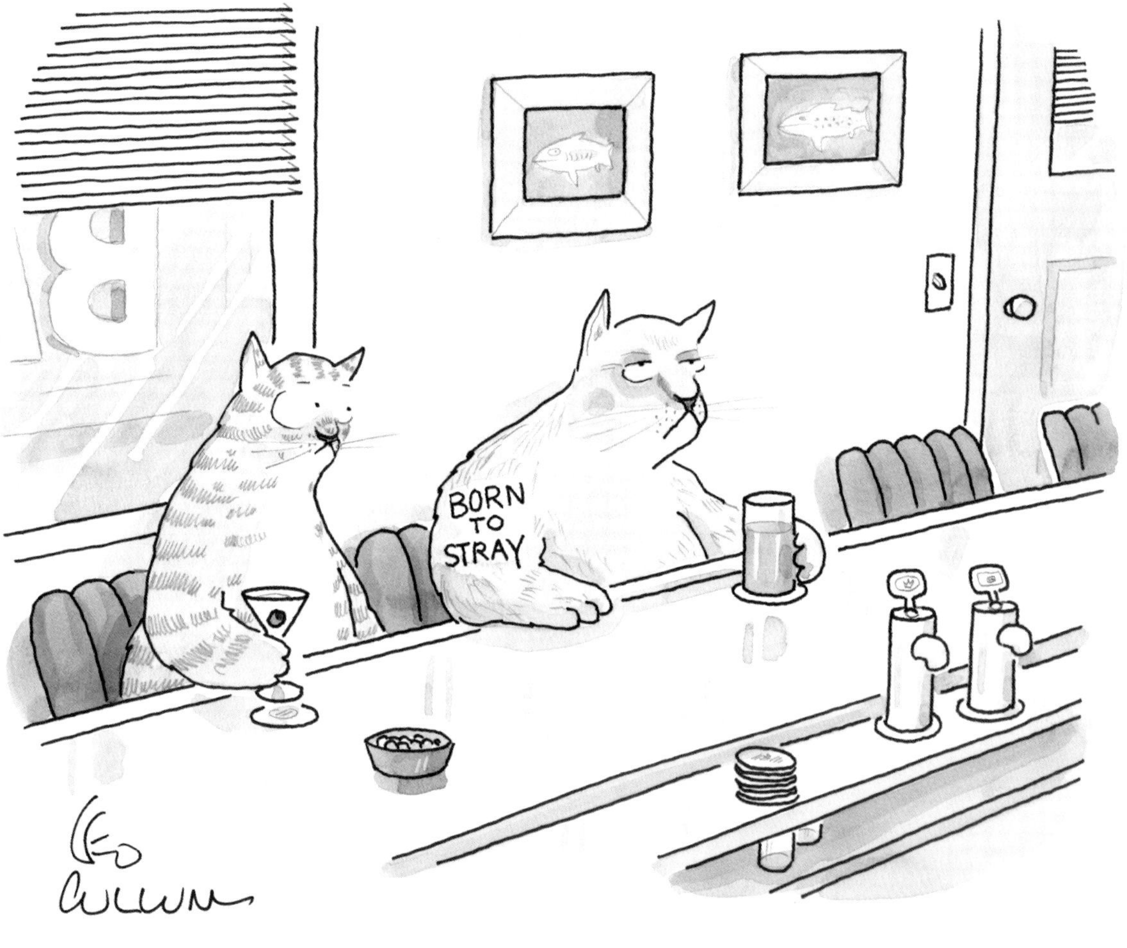
BORN TO STRAY

"Housekeeping."

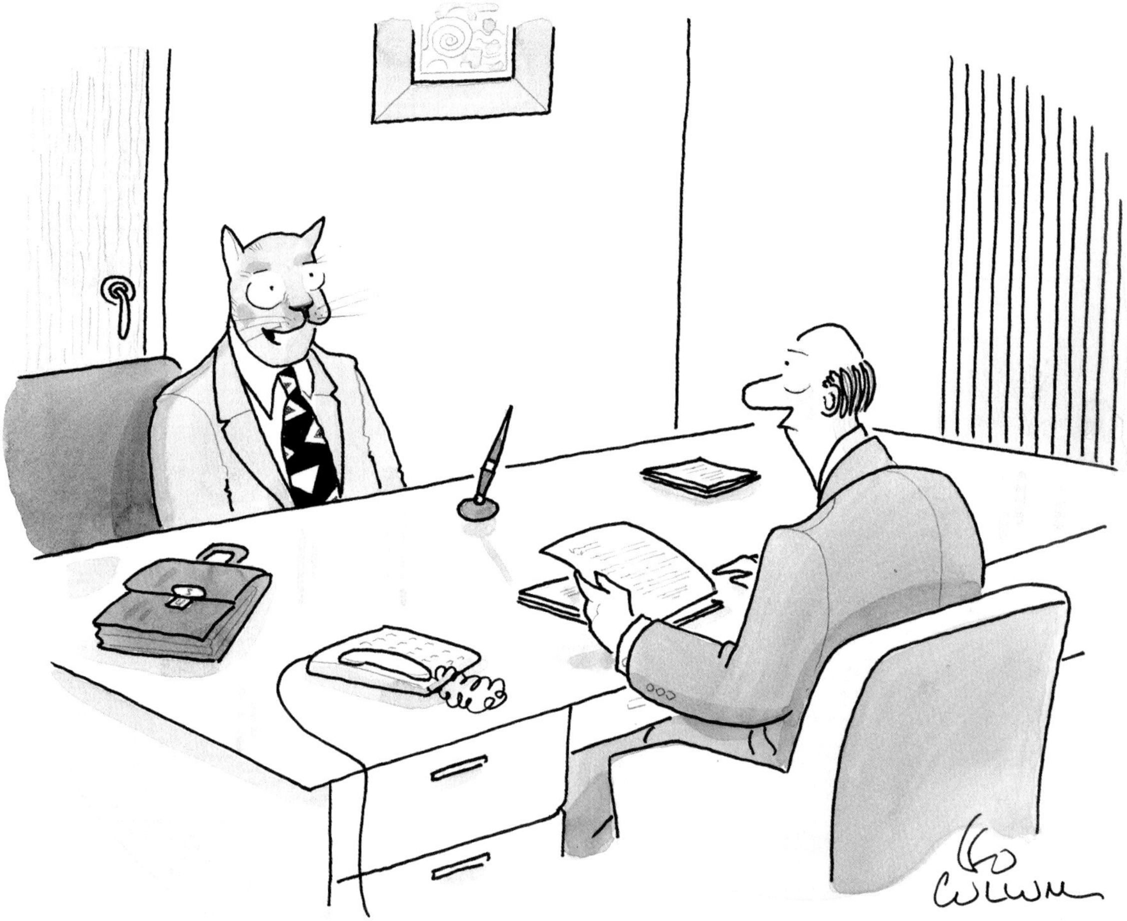
Leo Cullum

"I have a bachelor's degree from Columbia, an MBA from Stanford, six years experience, and I'm a hell of a mouser."

"You're completely screwed up."

"If you want me to show you a pas du chat, I'll show you a pas du chat."

"*This is humiliating. Couldn't you drop me a block from school?*"

"*Our anniversary! You remembered!*"

"I wish you bluebirds in the spring."

"Each of my previous books had nine editions."

"I'm a well-known food critic but I've never been able to turn it into cash."

"How did you get in here?"

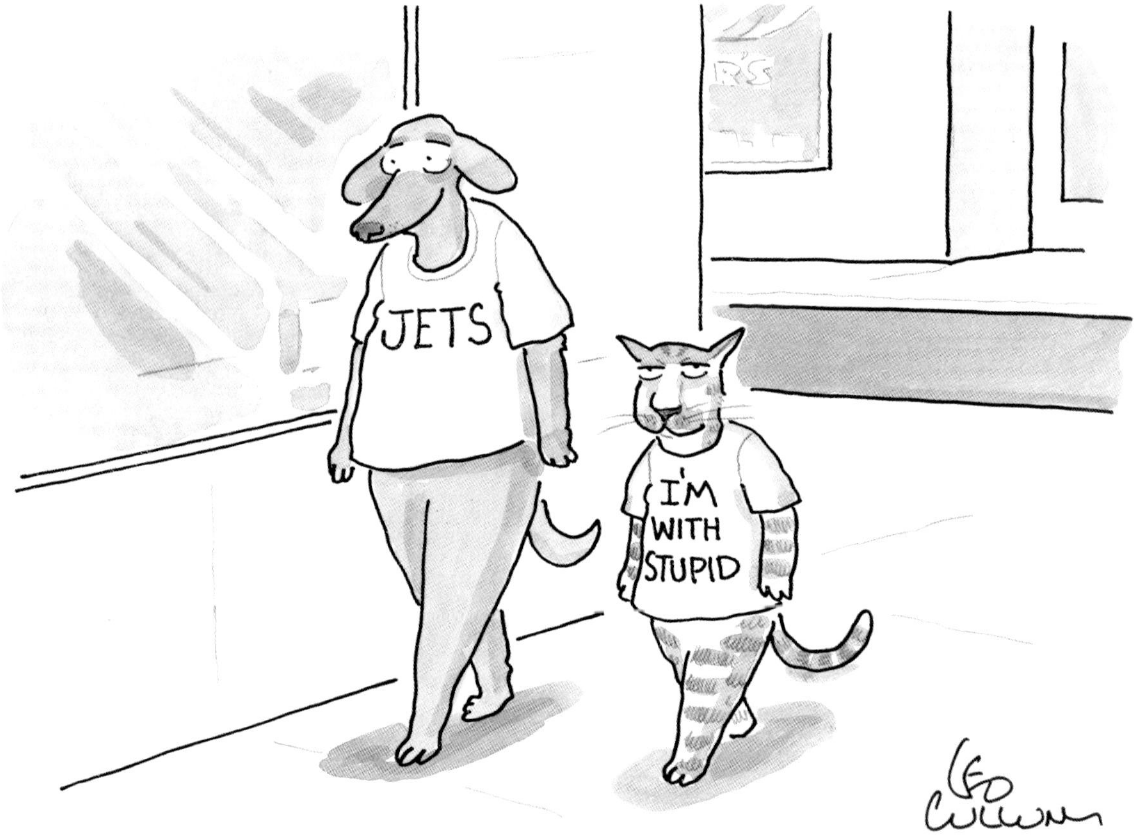
JETS
I'M
WITH
STUPID

"*If you must know, Jimmy, you came from a box in front of the market. It said, 'free kittens.'*"

"Pianissimo! Pianissimo!"

"Nora, what's this business with the cat?"

"And on the fifth day the Lord said, 'Let there be cats,' and there were cats."

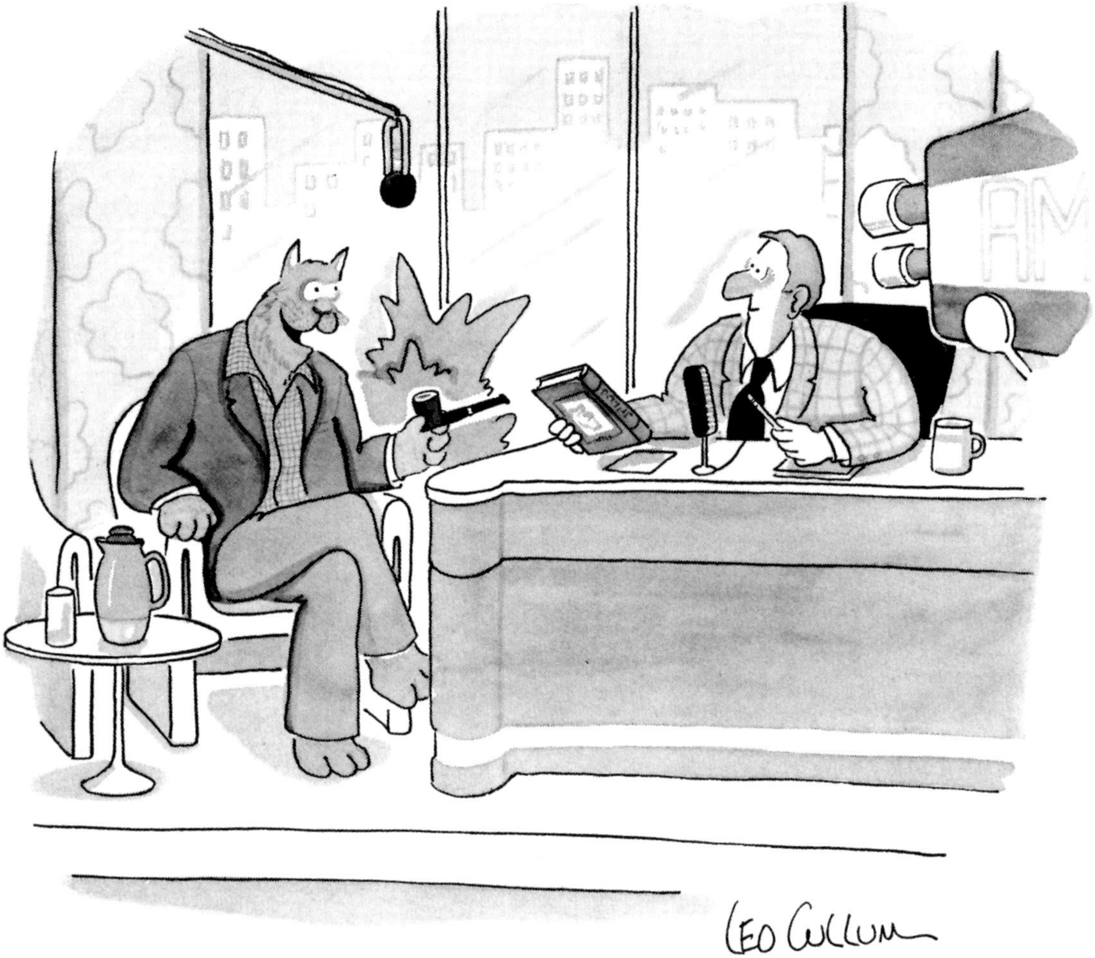
LEO CULLUM

"I know a lot of people will say, 'Oh, no—not another book about cats.'"

"Hey! Your ad said 'non-smoker'!"

THE CAT THAT ATE THE CANARY

THE CAT THAT DIDN'T EAT THE CANARY

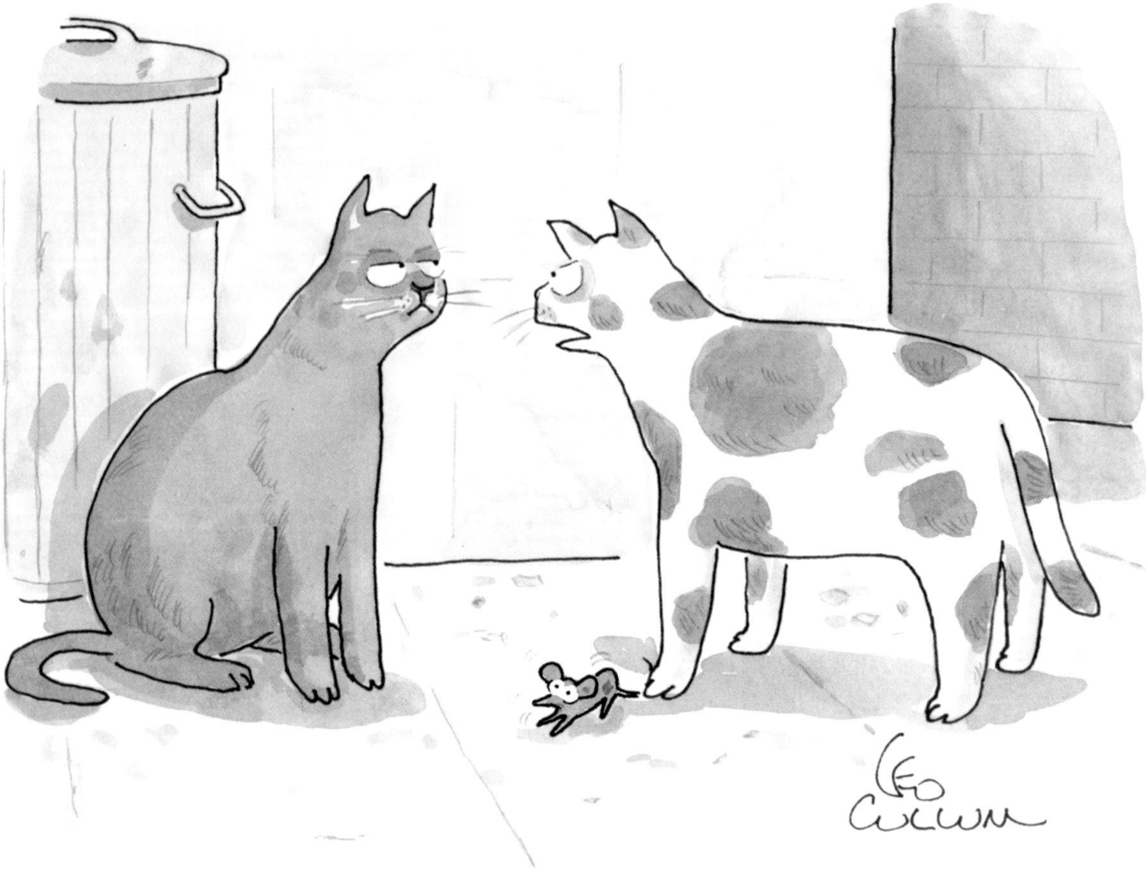
Leo Cullum

"You had a mouse for lunch? Why does that not surprise me?"

"I was in mergers and acquisitions but right now I'm a stray."

"If I had to give a reason it would be a combination of your poor performance and my allergies."

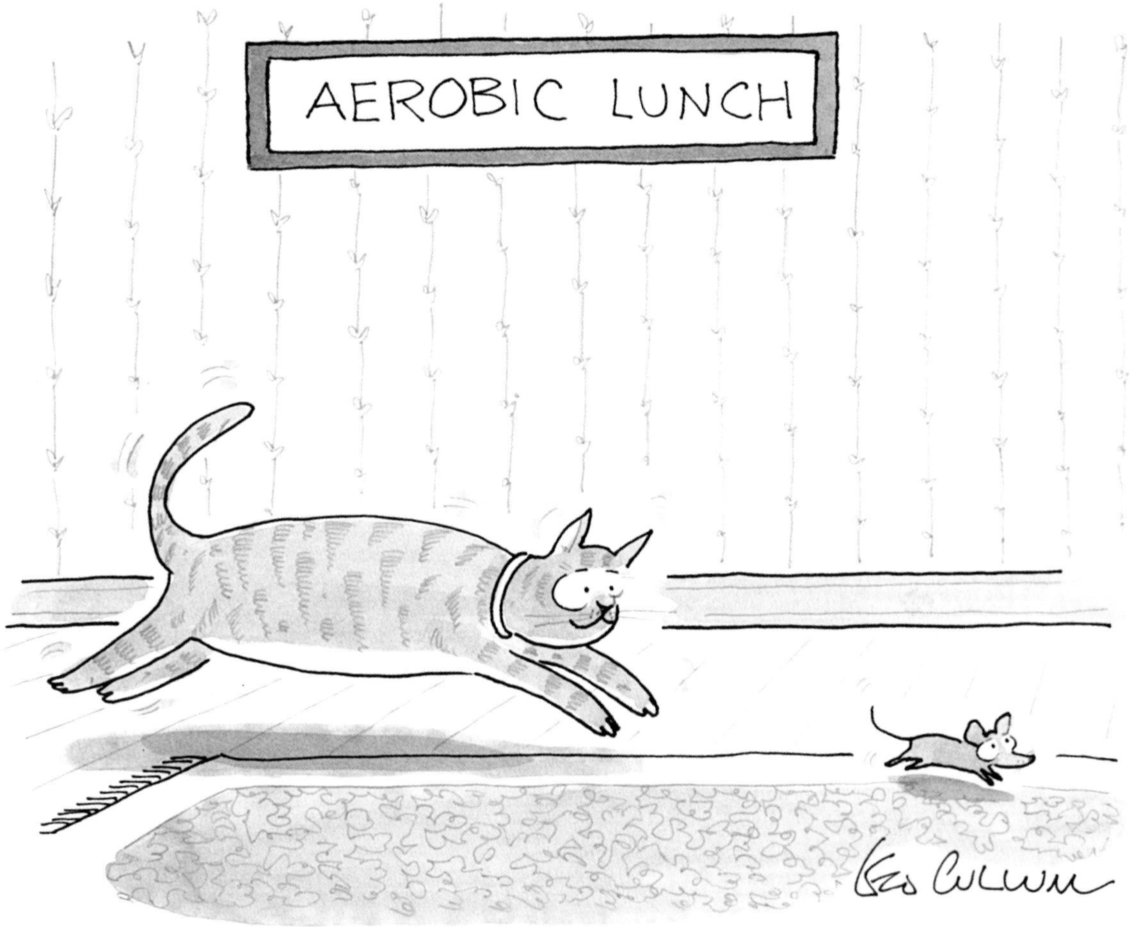
AEROBIC LUNCH
Leo Cullum

"*I'm being tracked by satellite.*"

"Is three blind mice one wish or three?"

"You're lucky. Dogs are easy to draw."

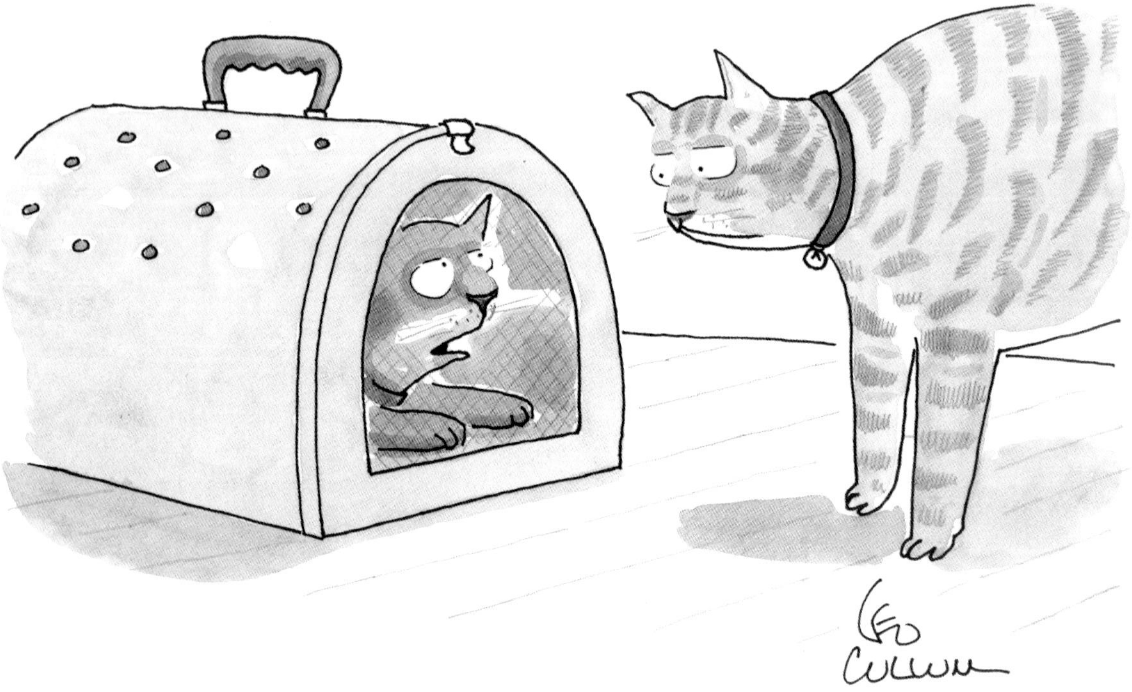
LEO
CULLUM

"I try to drink a lot of water, stay up and get right on L.A. time, and never eat the airline food."

"The deal looks cut-and-dried to me but Haskins smells a rat."

"*I'm sorry, Edward. I suddenly realized I'm not a cat person.*"

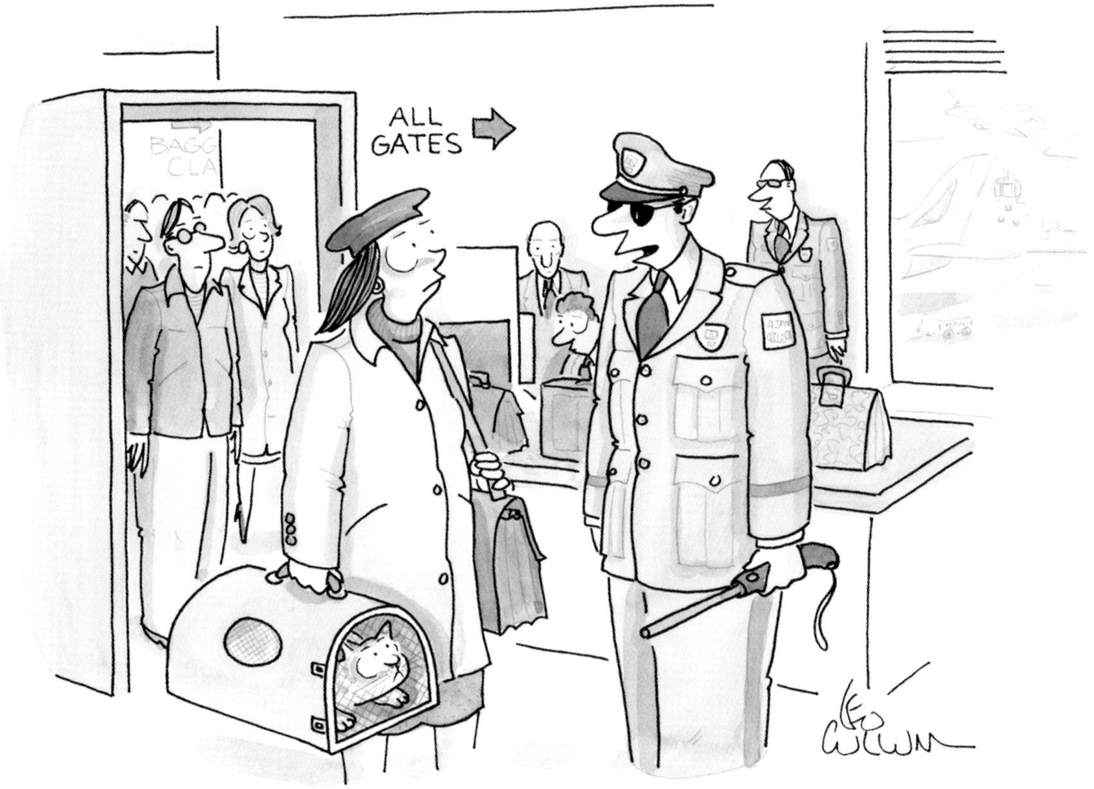
ALL
GATES

"We'll need to declaw the cat."

"It just comes naturally, I have good people skills."

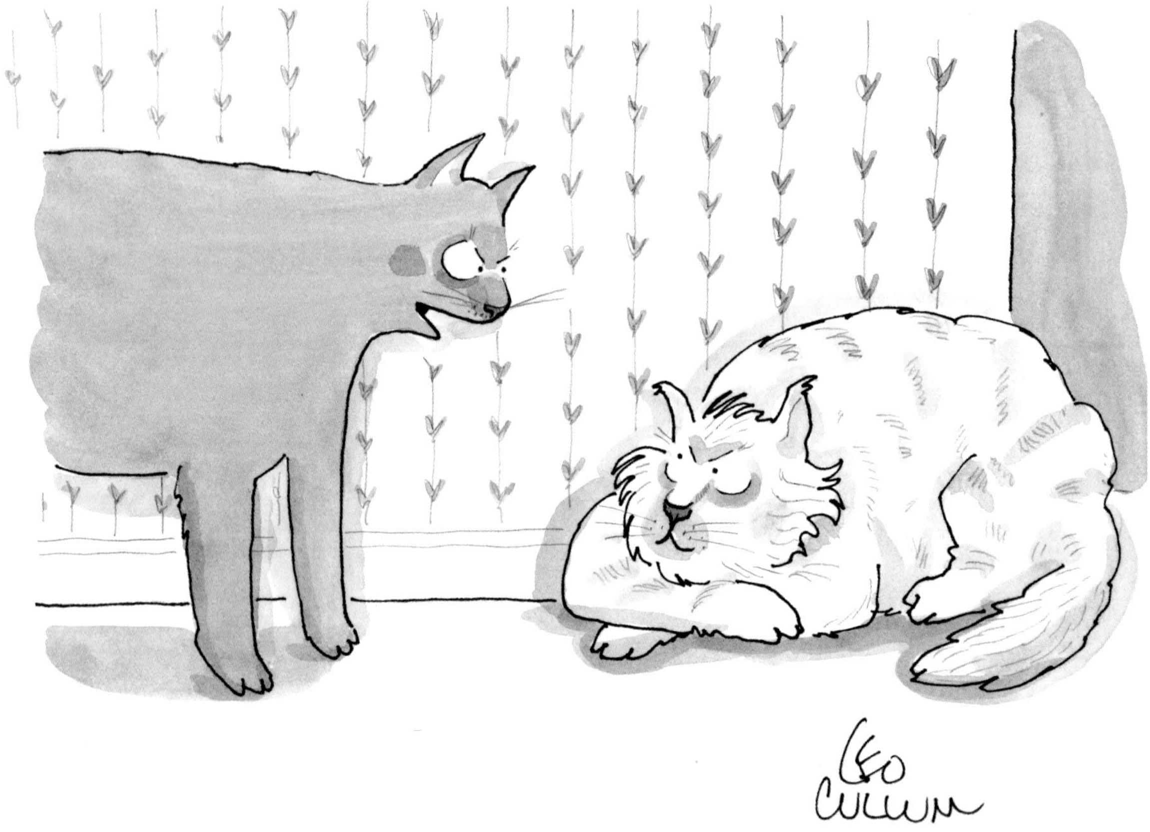
LEO CULLUM

"My friends warned me you were a different breed of cat."

"You will note that their ability to comprehend, assess, and process information increases dramatically when Professor Podhertz throws in the cat."

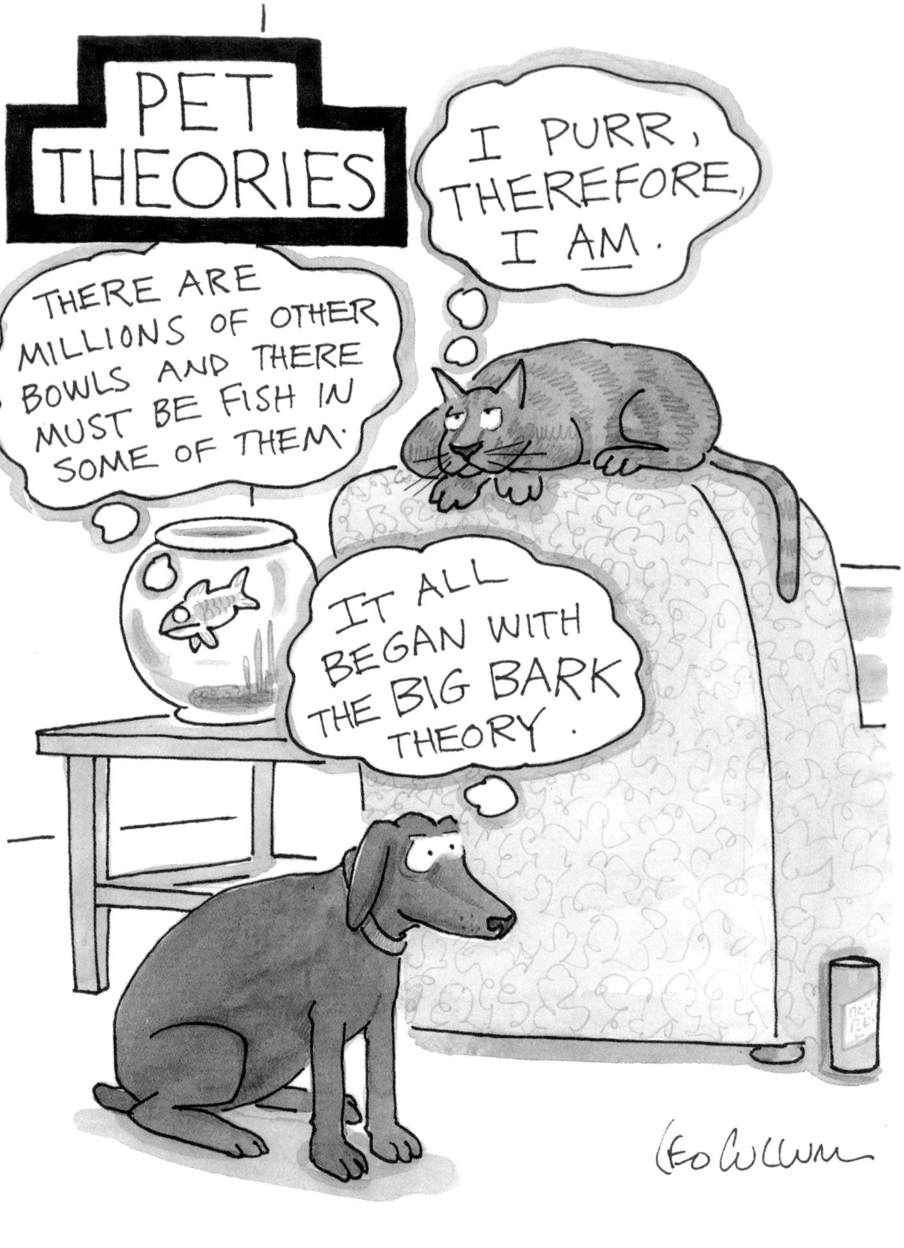
PET THEORIES
I PURR, THEREFORE, I AM.
THERE ARE MILLIONS OF OTHER BOWLS AND THERE MUST BE FISH IN SOME OF THEM.
IT ALL BEGAN WITH THE BIG BARK THEORY.
LEO CULLUM

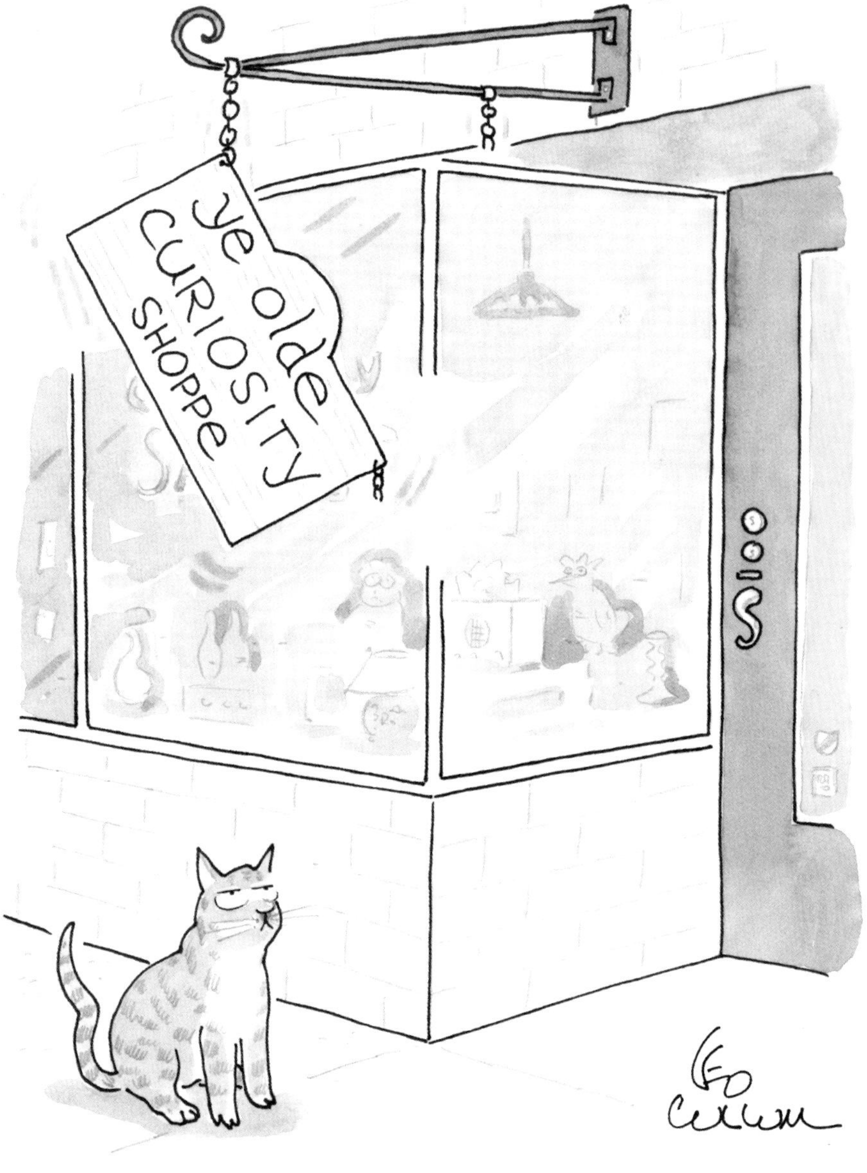
ye olde
CURIOSITY
SHOPPE

"The word you're looking for is 'rapprochement.'"

"*I love you both very much but I've got to find my real parents.*"

"What the hell went on around here while I was gone?"

"Yes, the market did advance this week, Rebecca, but we feel it's somewhat of a 'dead-cat bounce.'"

"It's not enough being a cat anymore. I want to be a fat cat."

"The thing is, we lived in L.A.,...we never even needed *mittens!"*

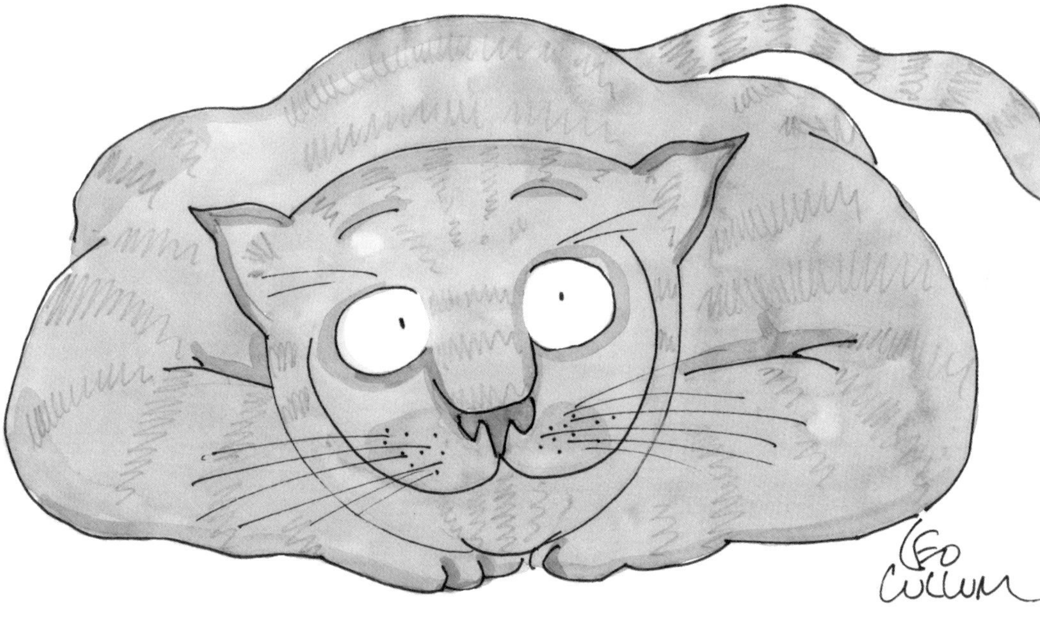
LEO CULLUM

THE CAT THAT ATE THE BLUEBIRD OF HAPPINESS

"It's curiosity."

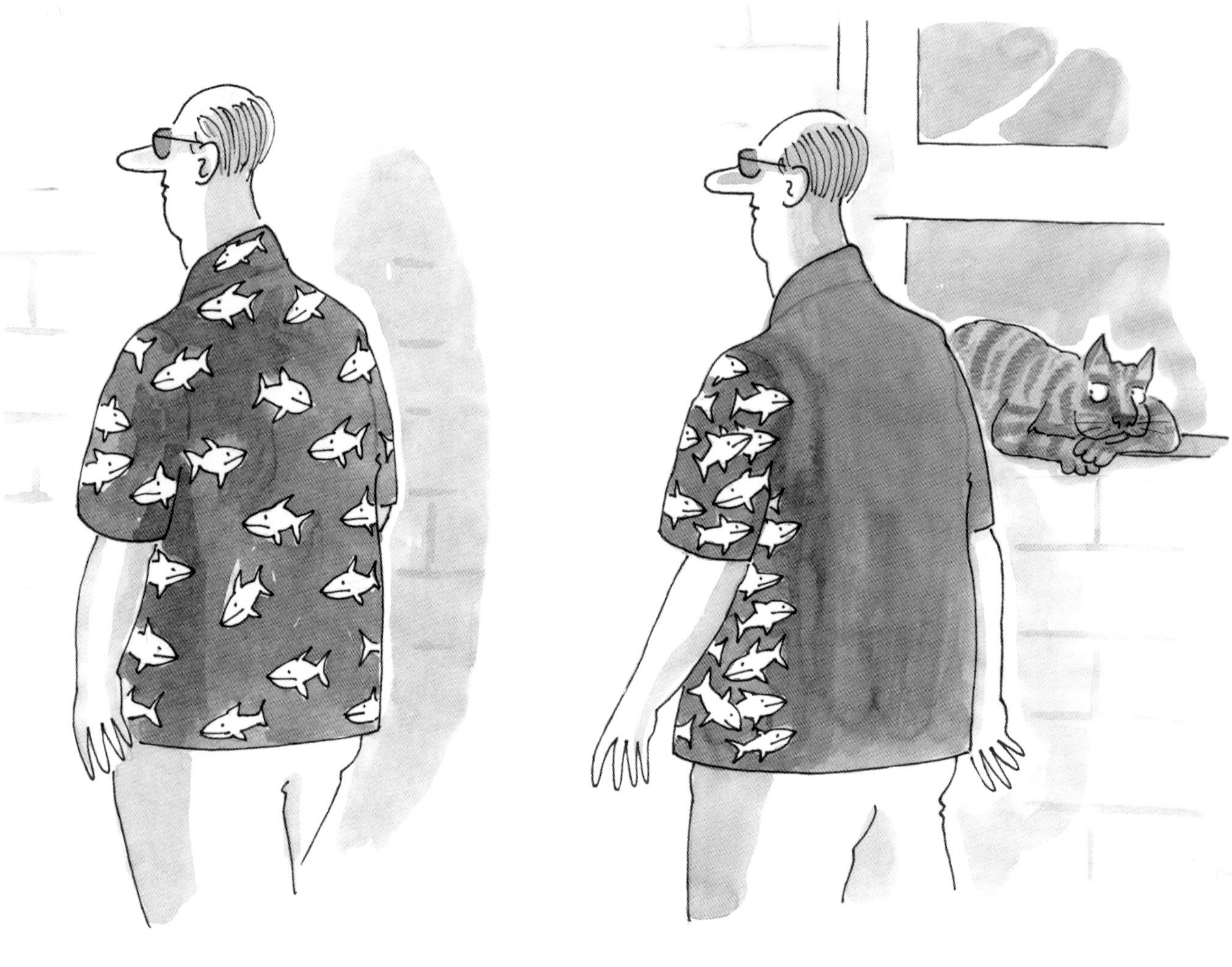

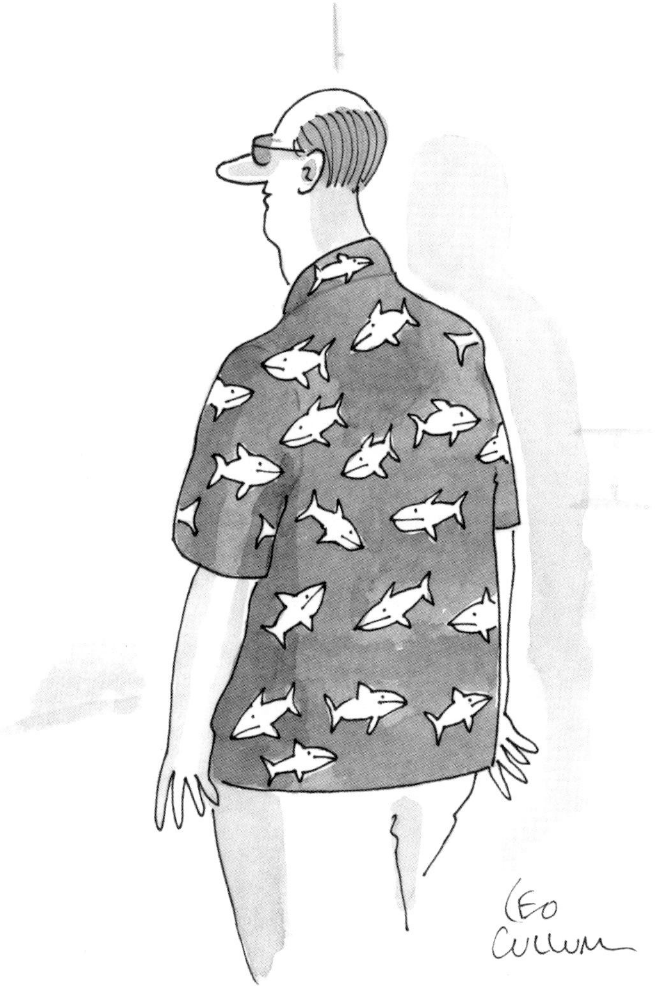
LEO CULLUM

"I tried dog food once. It tasted like chicken."

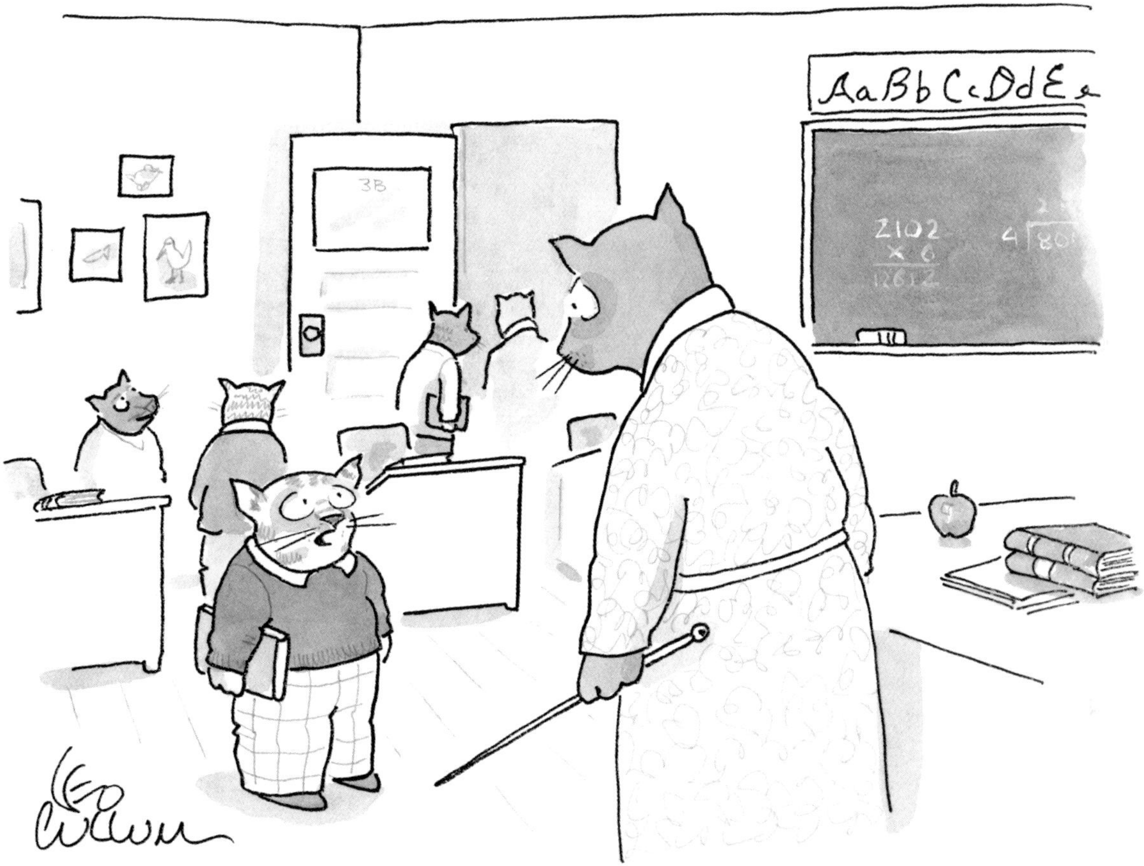
AaBbCcDdE
3B
2102
× 6

"My sister had my homework. The dog ate them both."

"*France has devalued the cat.*"

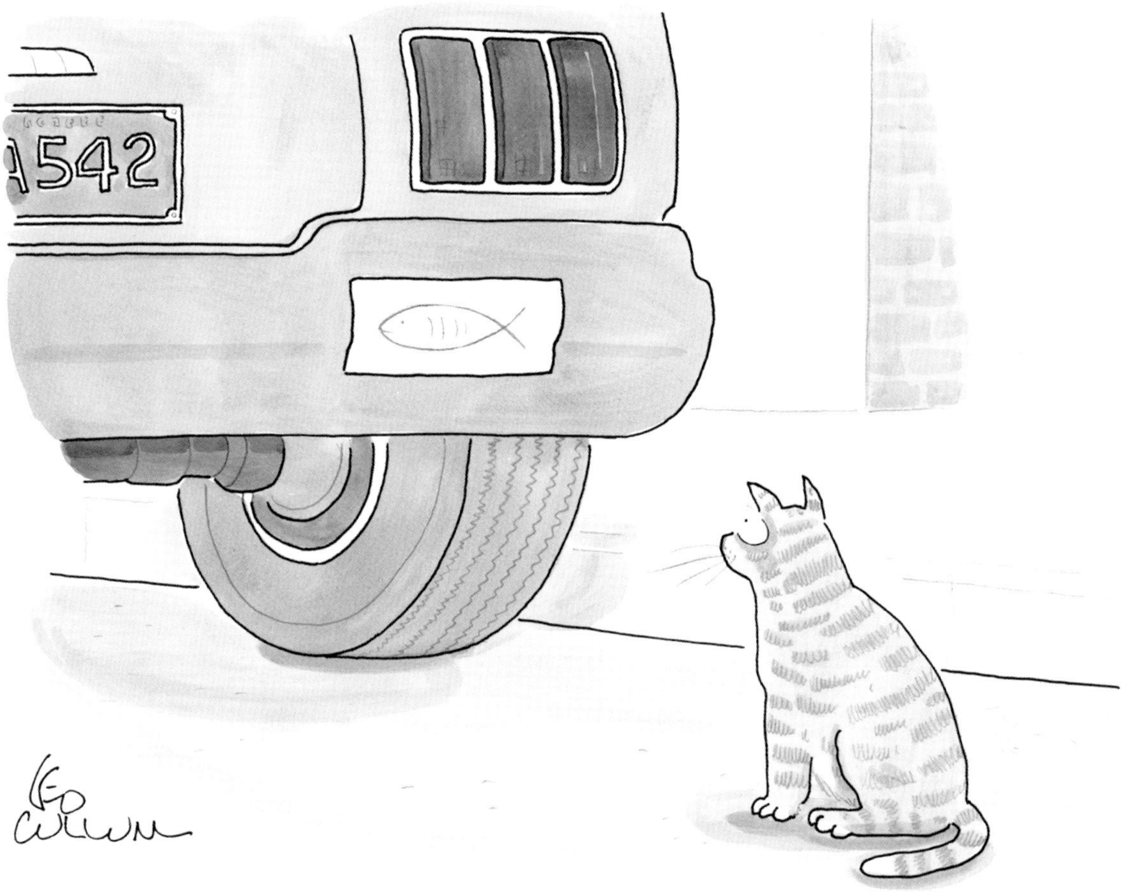
A542

"*Does this collar make me look fat?*"

"Most of all I love your vulnerability."

"You had coffee and the canary, right,…right?

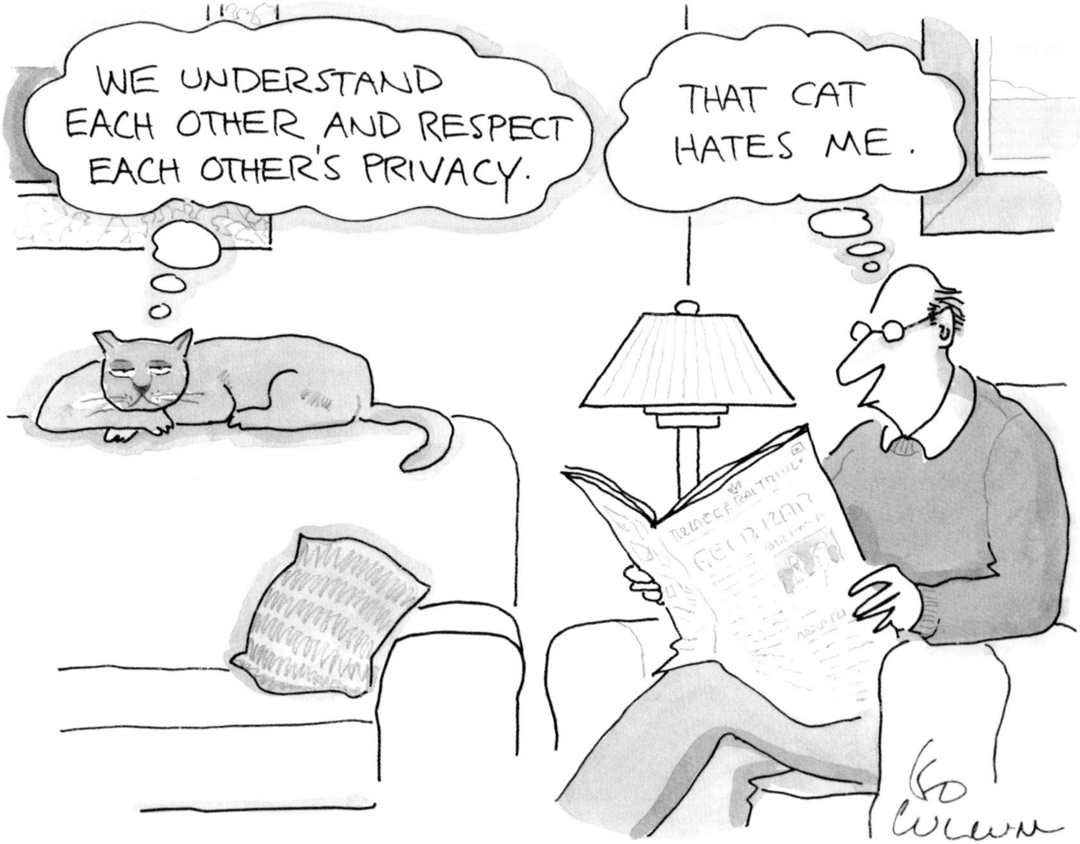
WE UNDERSTAND EACH OTHER AND RESPECT EACH OTHER'S PRIVACY.
THAT CAT HATES ME.

"I take no pleasure in it, Kaplowe, but I have to kill you and devour you. It's company policy."

"I'll come, if you quit wagging your tail."

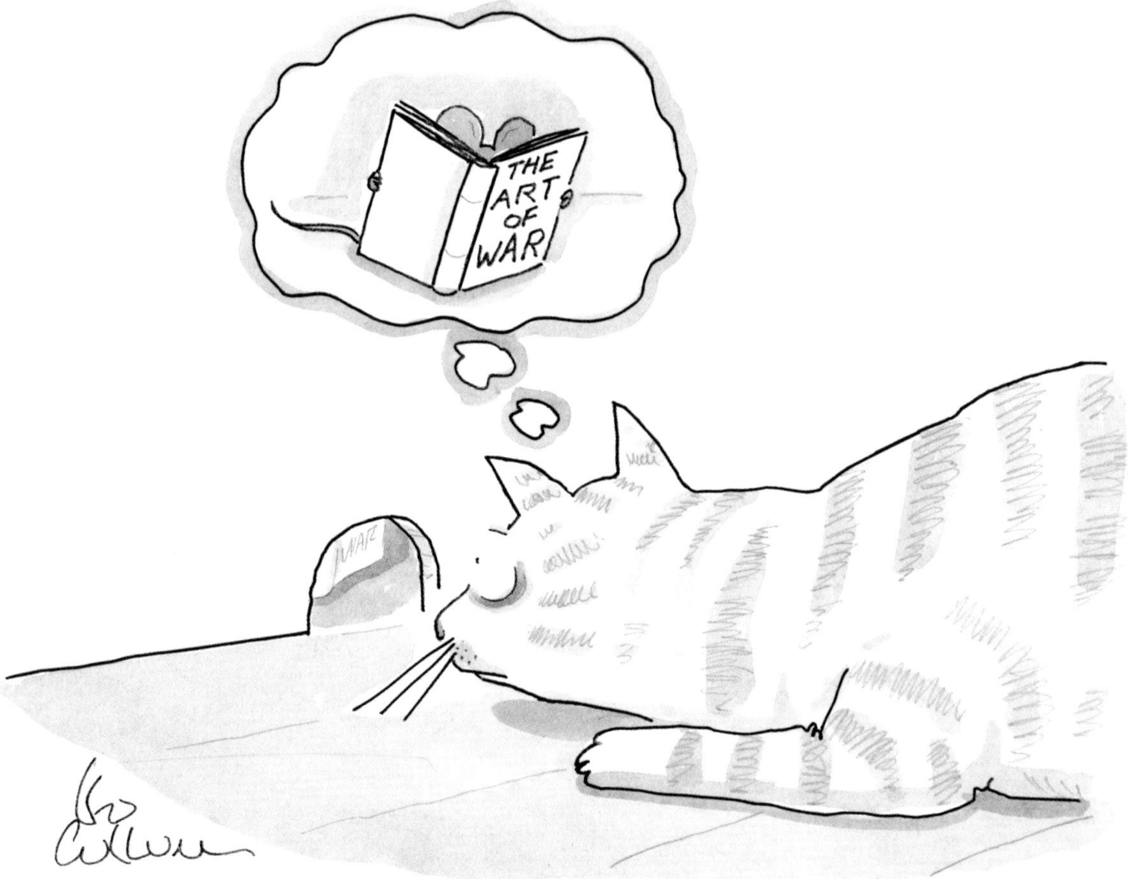
THE ART OF WAR

"If I weren't in the ACLU, I would never take your case."

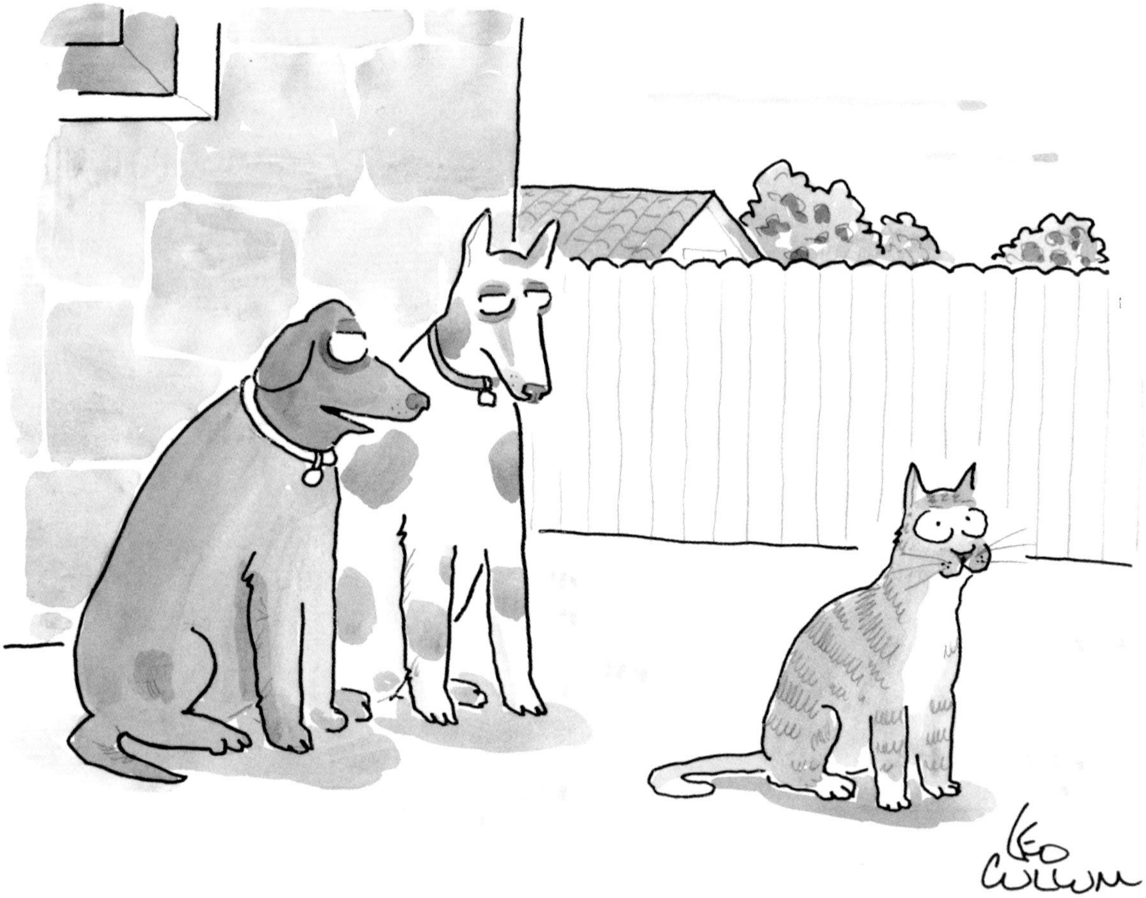
LEO CULLUM

"I'm certain it wasn't intellectual curiosity that killed the cat."

"*Whatever you do,…don't* scurry!"

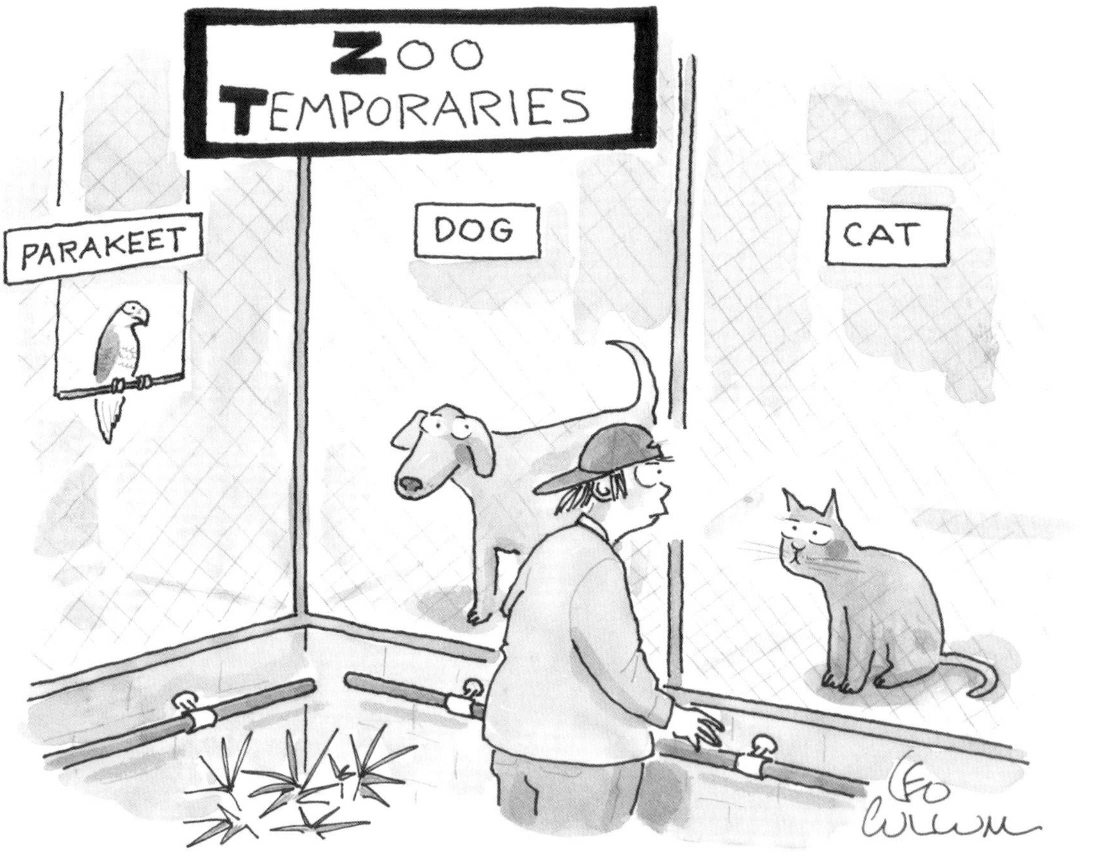
ZOO
TEMPORARIES
PARAKEET
DOG
CAT

"*I understand cats have three hundred words for kitty litter.*"

"It's nice, but is there room to swing a cat?"

"You really took Muffy and Scott and Todd down to the lake and let them go...honest? Have you got a note or something from them so I could be sure?"

"Bad news. We're on the Atkins diet."

"Cats! Can't live with them,...can't eat them."

"Mr. Cosgrove. Mouse in accounting!"

"The first eight times it was curiosity. The last time I was run over."

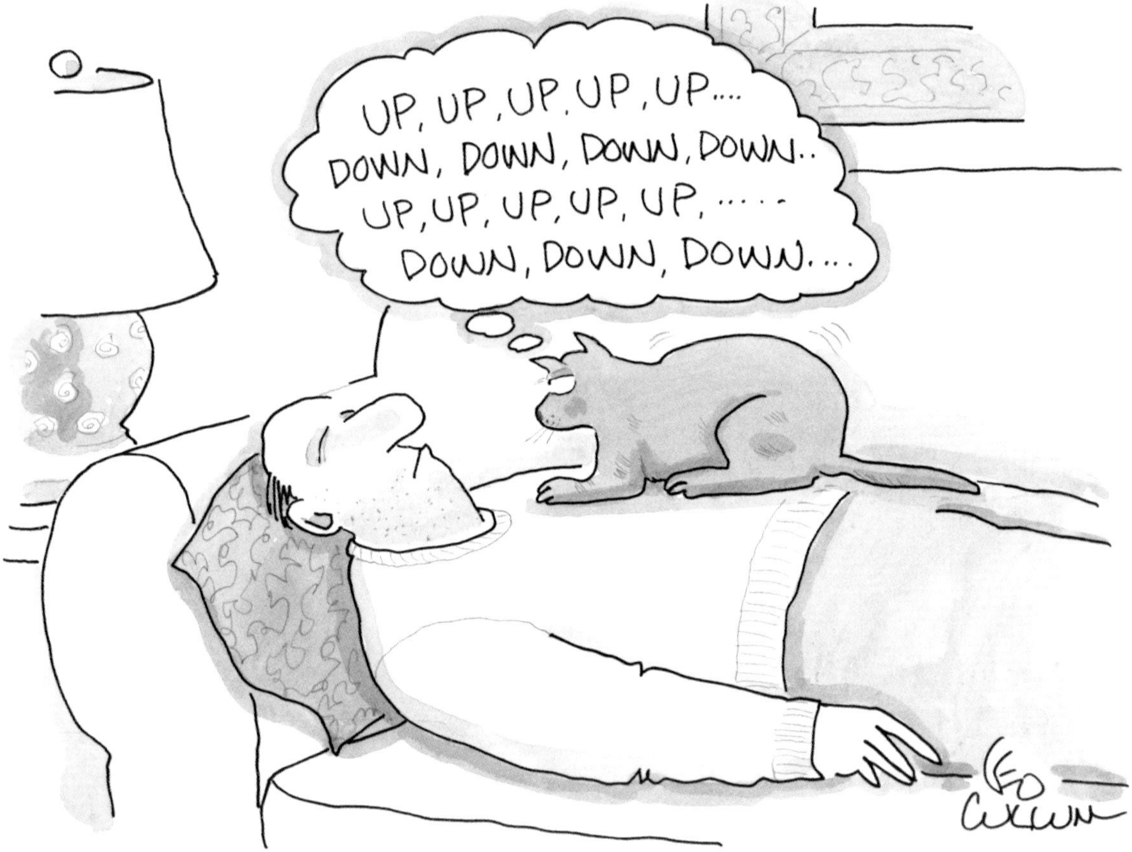
UP, UP, UP, UP, UP....
DOWN, DOWN, DOWN, DOWN..
UP, UP, UP, UP, UP, ...
DOWN, DOWN, DOWN....

"Maybe you just can't tell a joke."

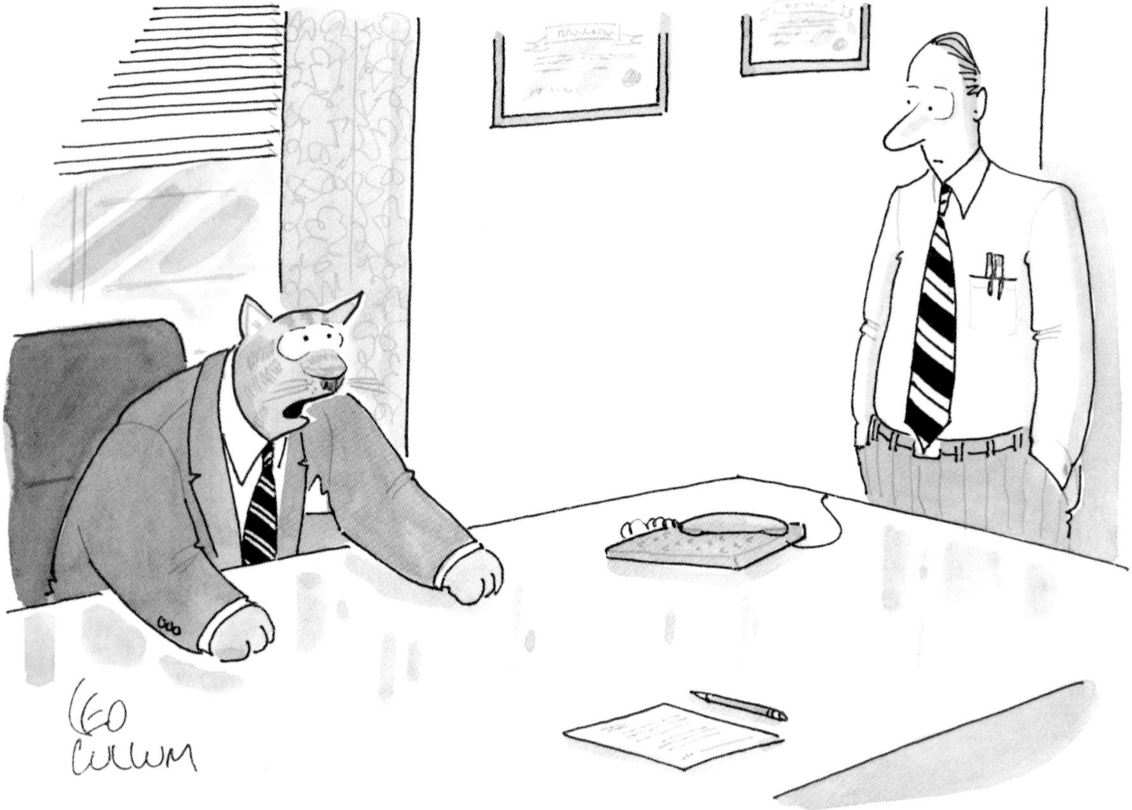
LEO CULLUM

"He had the pen in his hand and was about to sign the deal when I coughed up a hairball."

"You're light on your feet for a dog."

"I think big feet means he's going to be a big idiot."

"*Stock options won't do it. I'll also need a ball of yarn.*"

"I'm over my allergy attack and would like to try again."

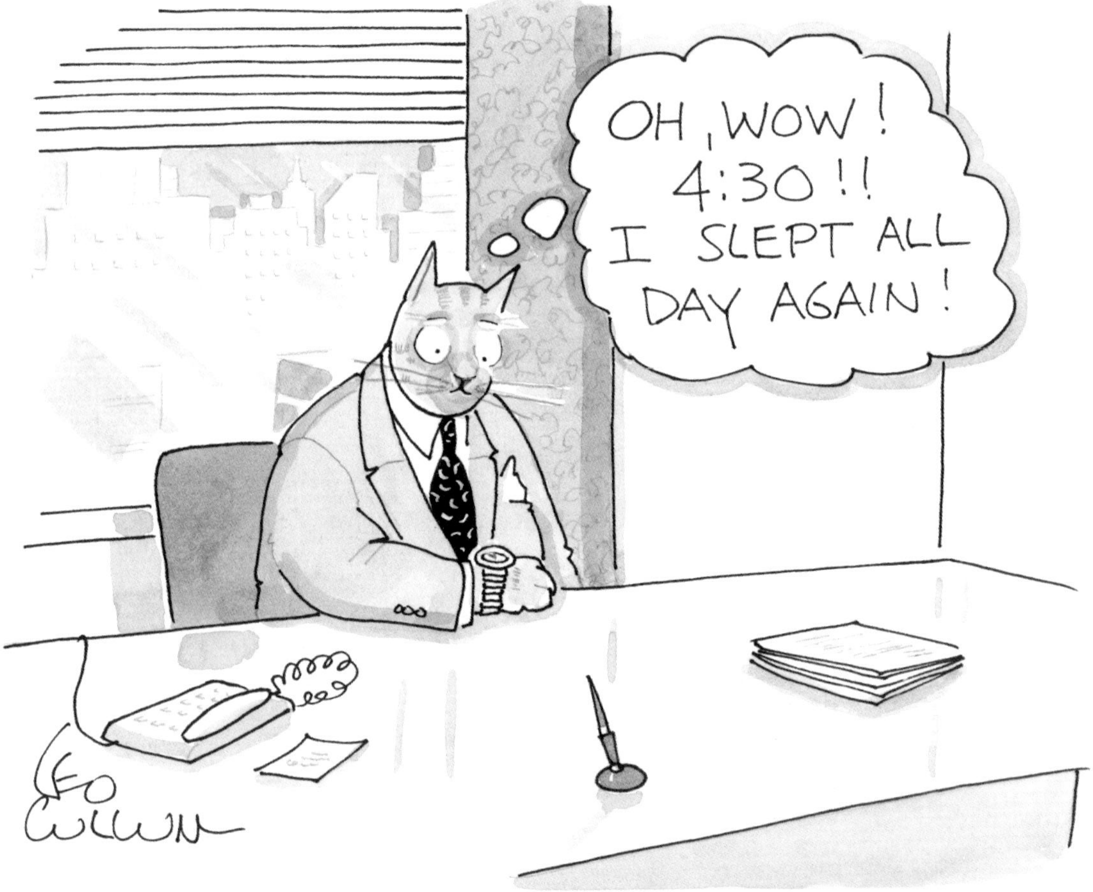
OH, WOW! 4:30!! I SLEPT ALL DAY AGAIN!
LEO CULLUM

"I had a 'birdie' on seven, a 'birdie' on eleven, and three more 'birdies' on eighteen. After that I was too full for lunch."

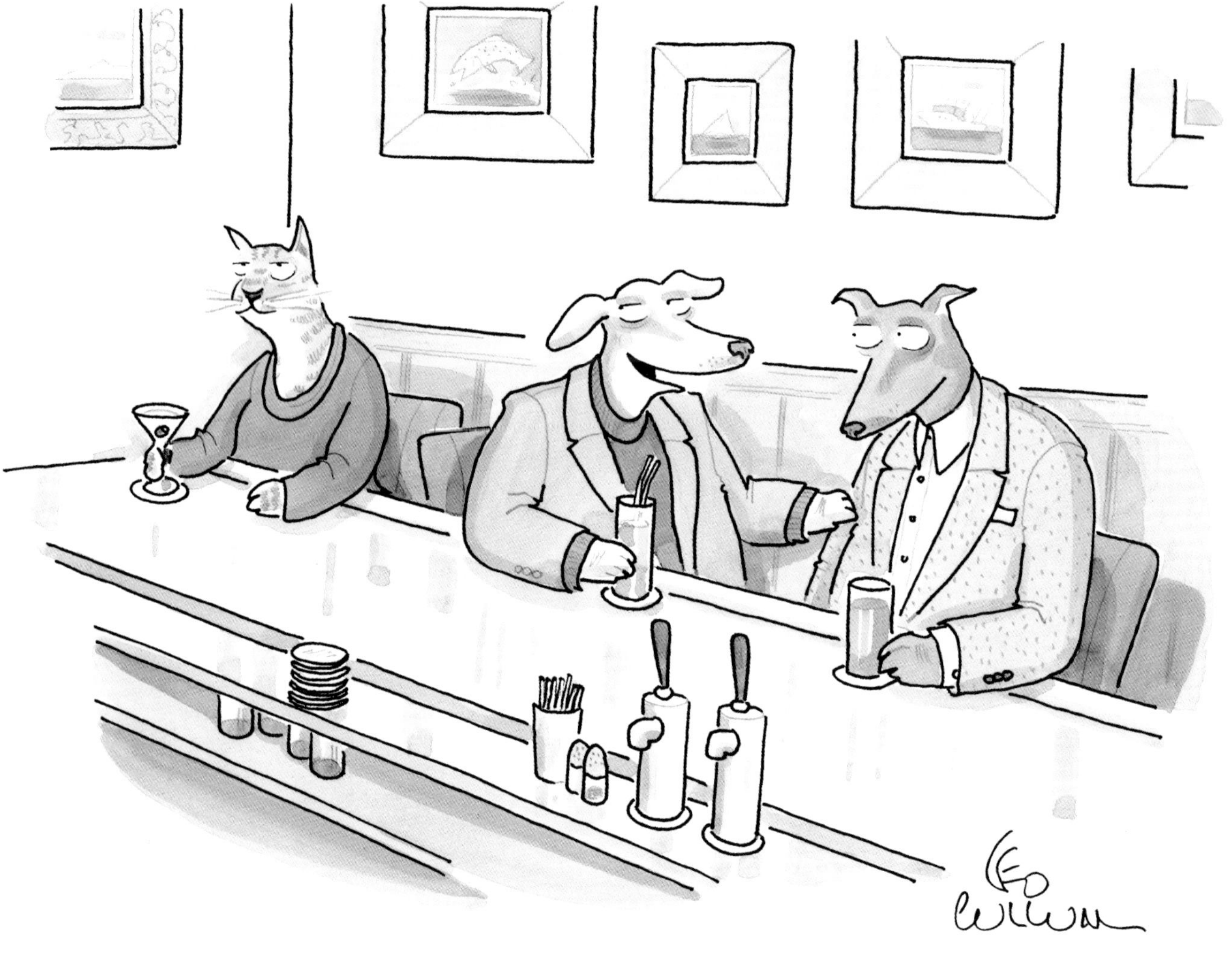

"I once kissed a cat. It was totally weird."

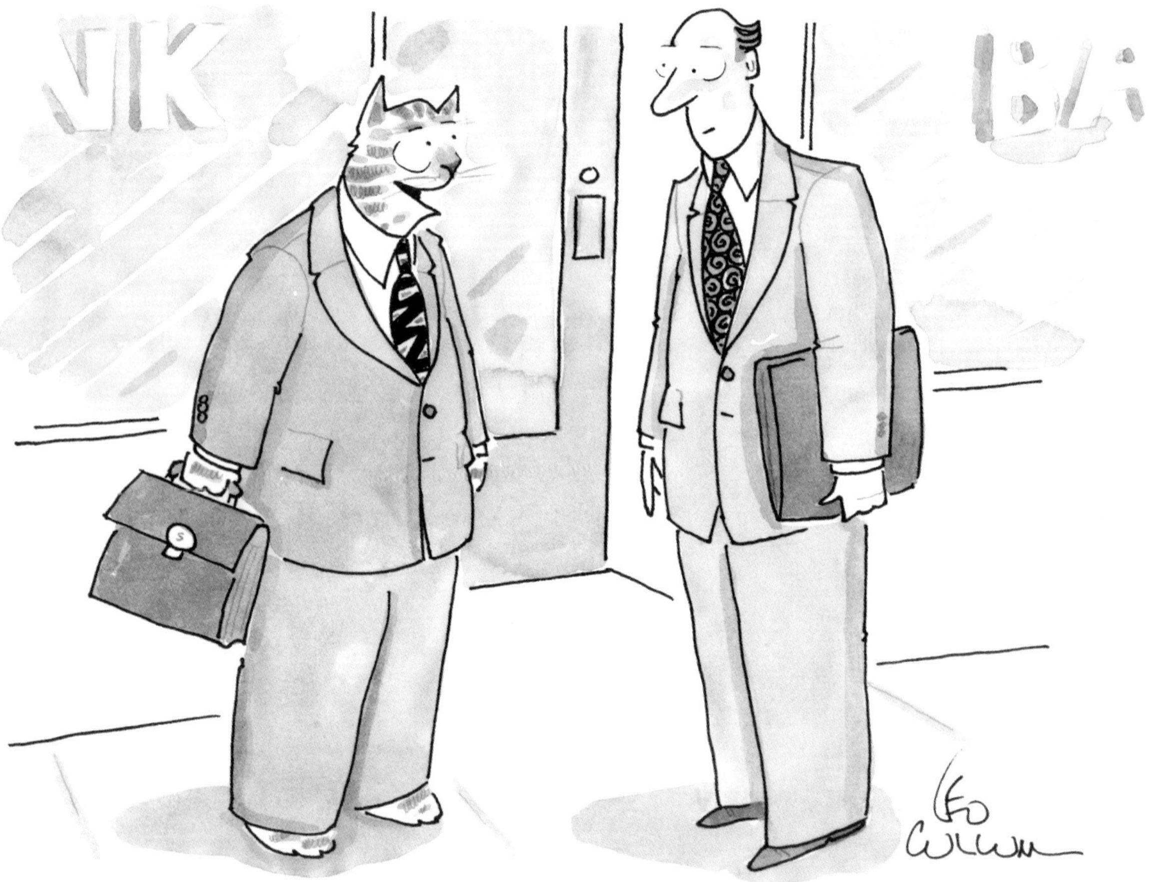
NK
BA

"I've been out of work three times this year but I always seem to land on my feet."

"Of course it's not a real bird. If it were a real bird we could eat it."

"No, we don't live in the city. We live on a boat."

"*You have two things to fear; fear itself and me.*"

"Whenever I sense an earthquake coming I close my eyes and pretend I'm napping."

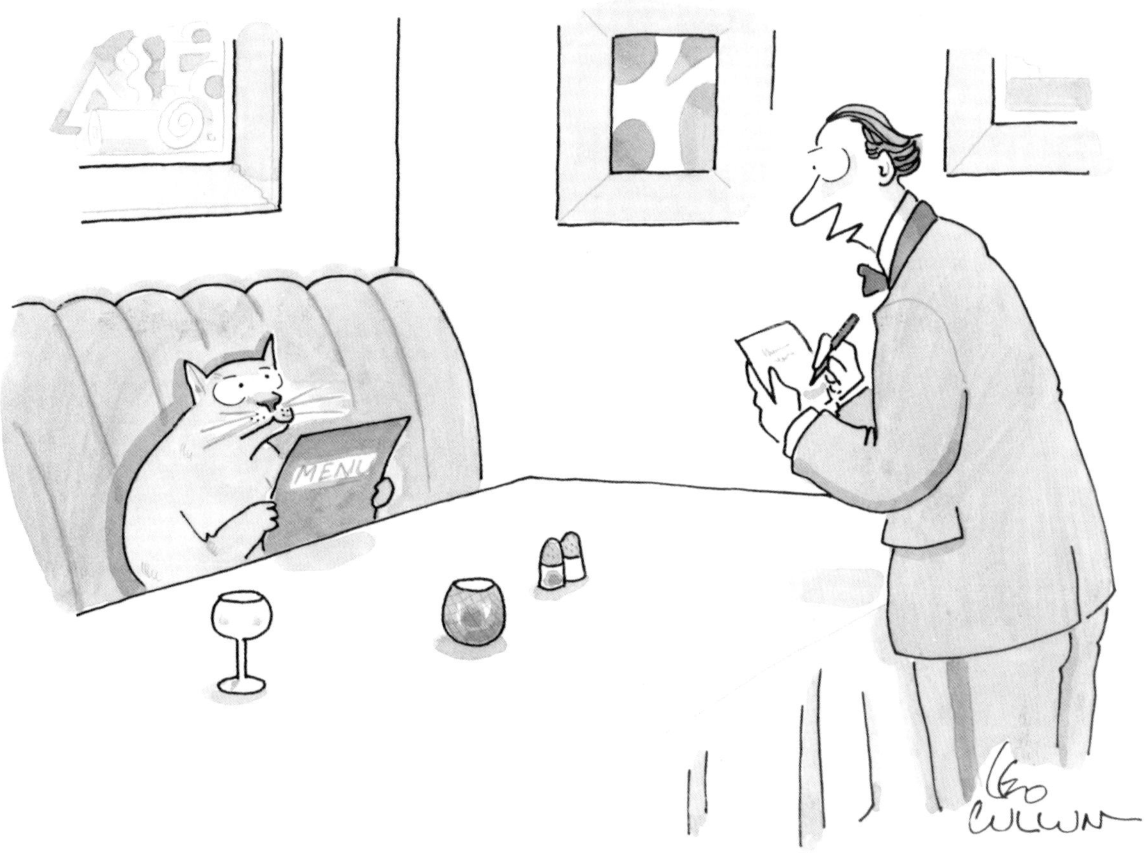
MENU

"We recommend red wine with mice and white wine with birds."

"Janet, cancel my Guido's reservation. I'll be having lunch in the office."

"Intellectually, I couldn't agree more."

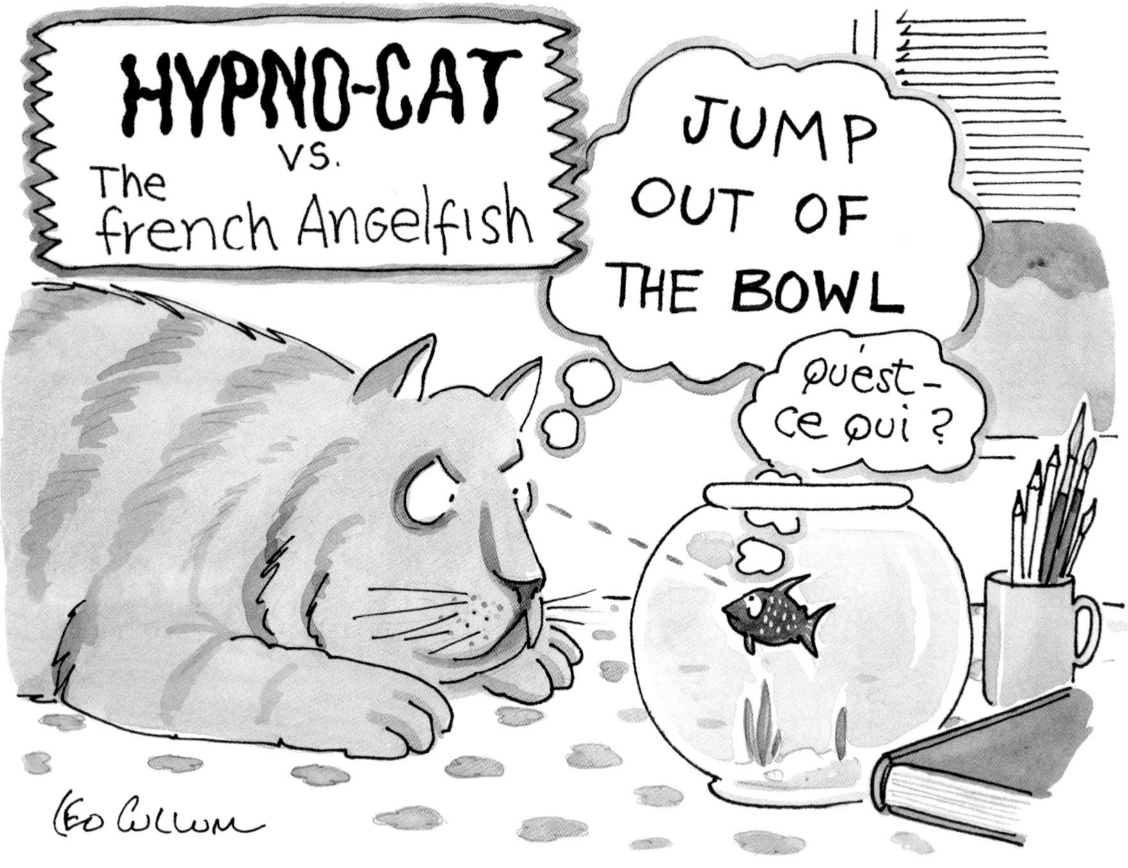
HYPNO-CAT
VS.
The french Angelfish
JUMP OUT OF THE BOWL
Qu'est-ce qui ?
LEO CULLUM

"Purr, goddammit!"

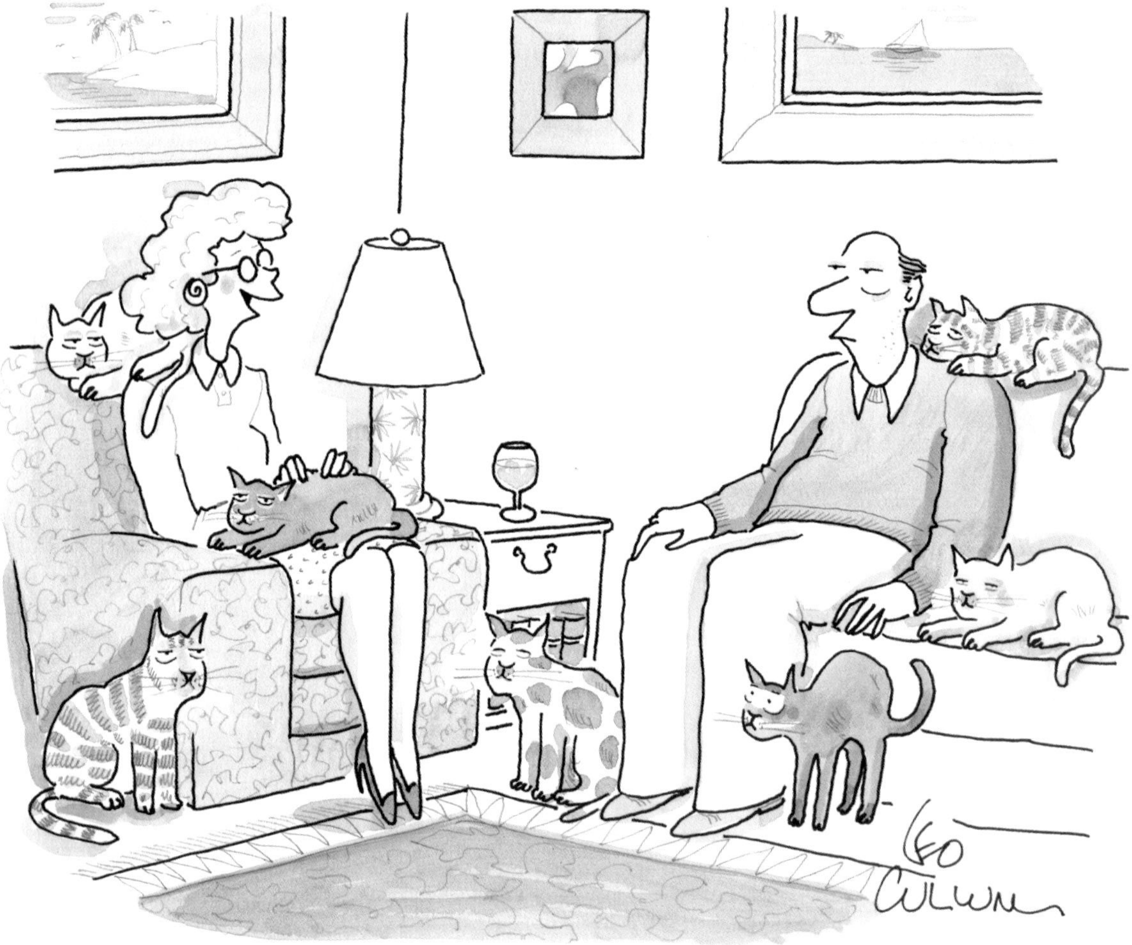
Leo Cullum

"A kitten for your thoughts."

"Is your regret that there were three of them or that they were blind?"

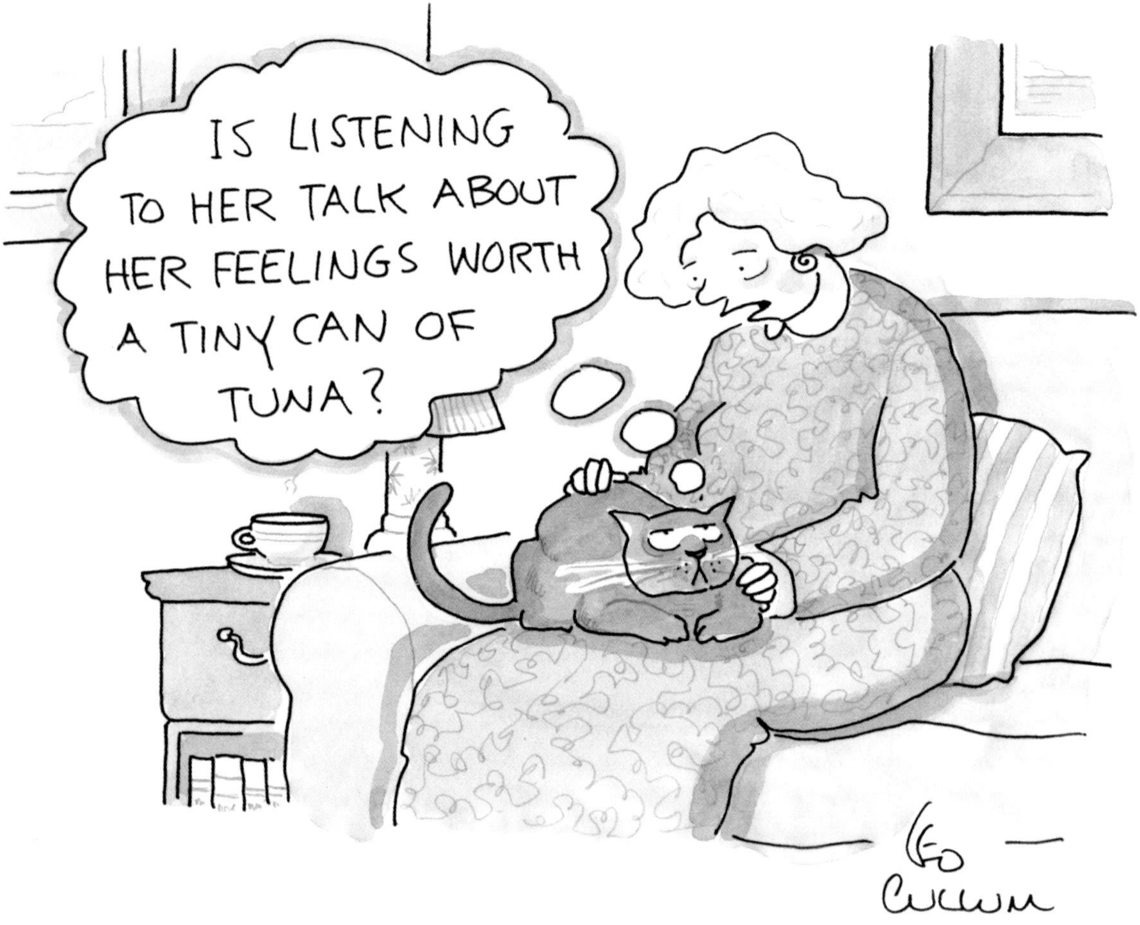
IS LISTENING TO HER TALK ABOUT HER FEELINGS WORTH A TINY CAN OF TUNA?
LEO CULLUM

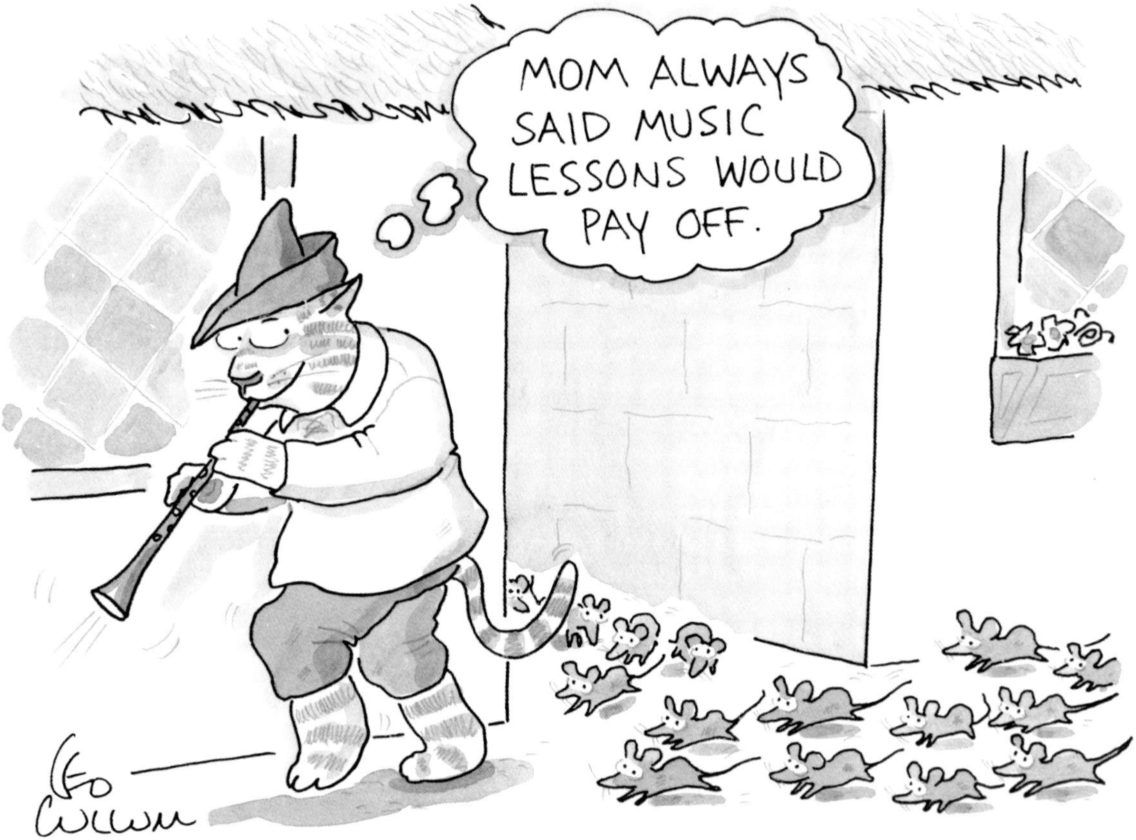
MOM ALWAYS SAID MUSIC LESSONS WOULD PAY OFF.

"Mouse jerky?"

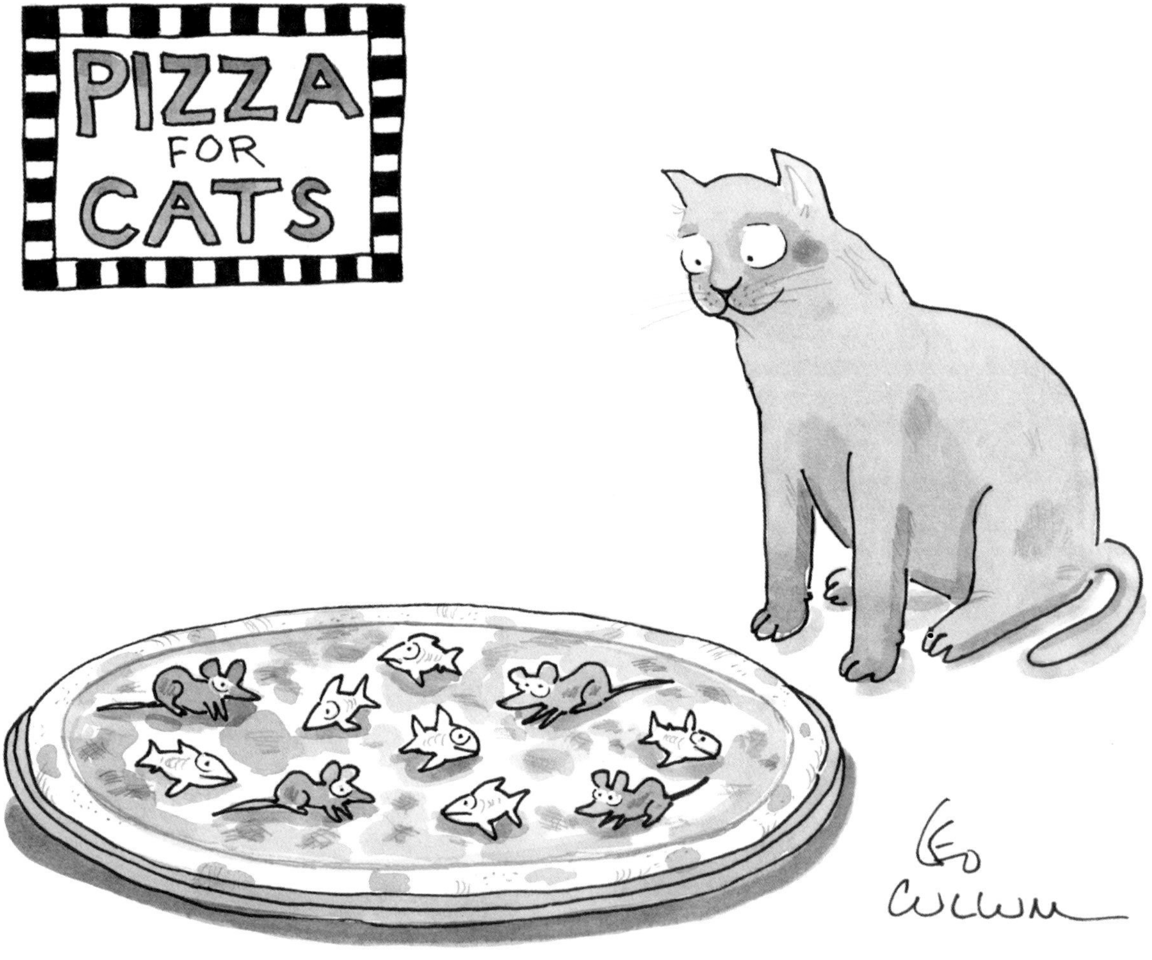
PIZZA
FOR
CATS

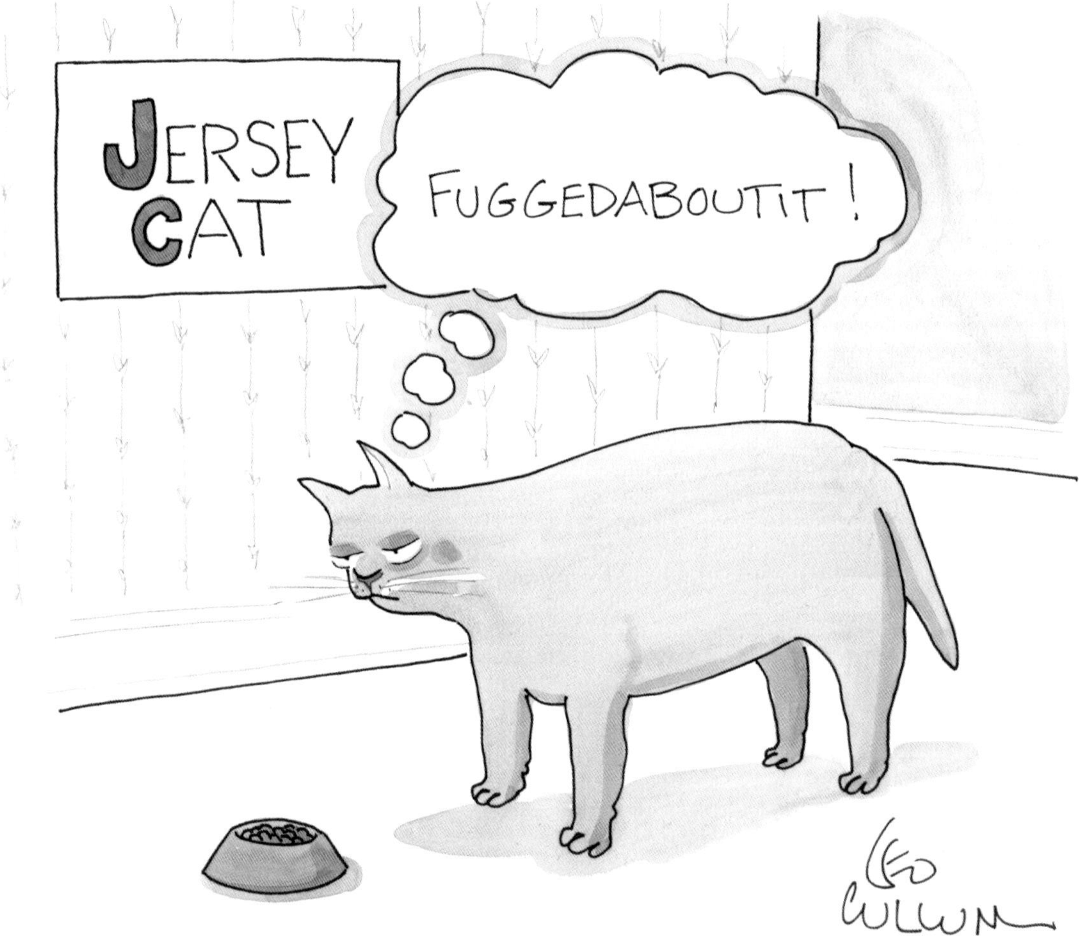
JERSEY CAT
FUGGEDABOUTIT!
LEO CULLUM

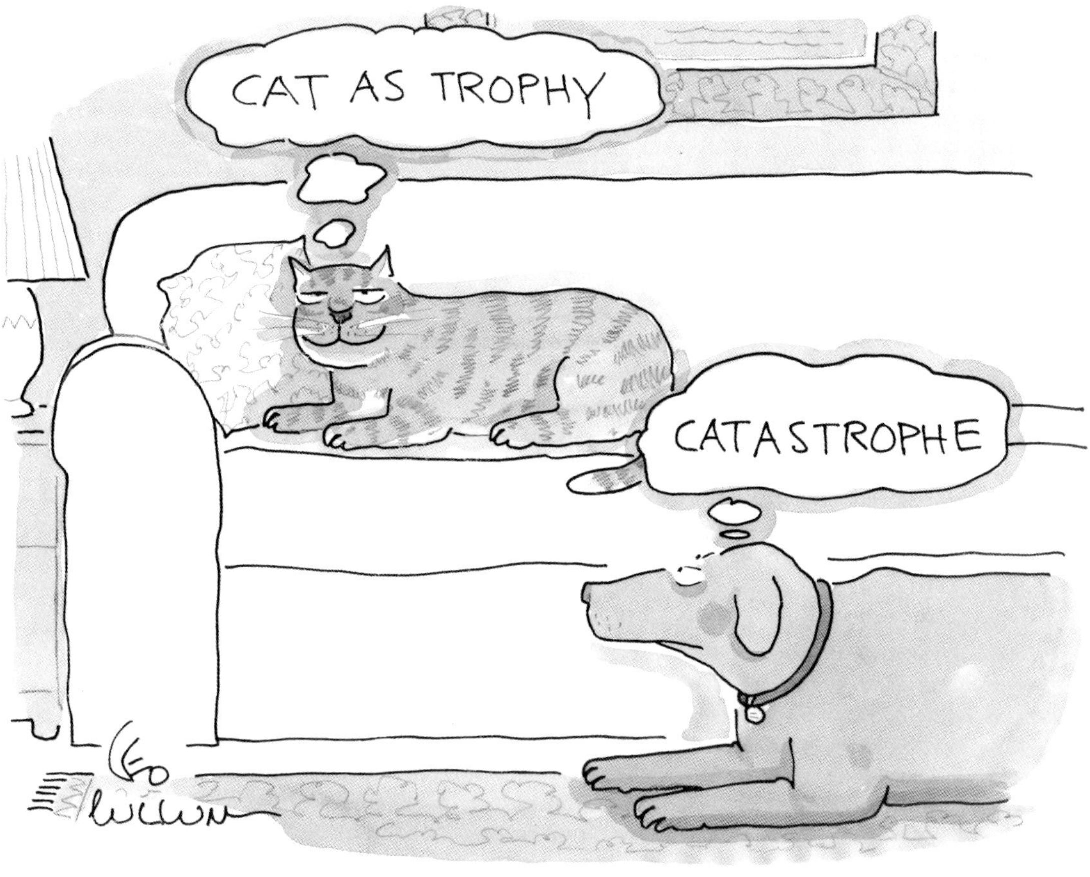
CAT AS TROPHY
CATASTROPHE

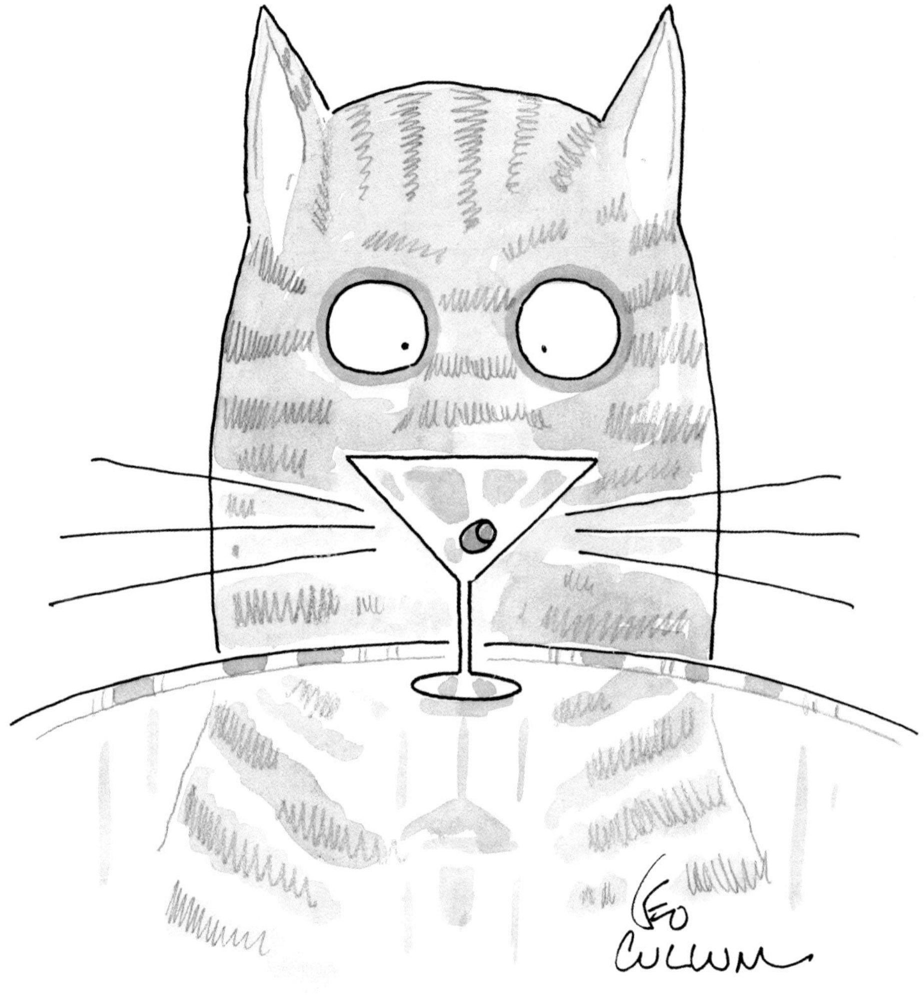
LEO CULLUM